425

A 2 (or 4) CS
100-125
Books 4 GT
95-130
(Mass)

LONG JOHN SILVER (V. Starrett) — This sonnet appears here for the first time in print. It was written in 1913.

TO R. L. S. (R. R. Greenwood) — From *The Overland Monthly*, December, 1913.

ROBERT LOUIS STEVENSON (E. T. Scheffauer) — From *The Book News Monthly*,— 1914; reprinted in *The Literary Digest*, September 19, 1914.

TO ROBERT LOUIS STEVENSON (E. C. Litsey) — From *Spindrift*, Louisville, Ky., 1915.

FRIEND O' MINE (S. Chalmers) — From *The Medical Pickwick*, Vol. I, No. 1, 1915.

THE DEATH OF FLINT (S. Chalmers) — First printed in the *New York Times*.

ROBERT LOUIS STEVENSON (S. Chalmers) — From *Munsey's Magazine*, May, 1916.

SAINT R. L. S. (S. N. Cleghorn) — From *Portraits and Protests*, 1917.

ON CERTAIN CRITICS OF STEVENSON (V. Starrett) — Written in 1917, this sonnet is here for the first time printed.

SAMOA AND R. L. S. (J. E. Middleton) — From *Sea Dogs and Men at Arma*, 1918.

THE TRAVELLERS (M. Monahan) — From the Sun Dial column of the *New York Evening Sun*, August 20, 1919.

A HOUSE IN SARANAC (G. S. Seymour)— Appears for the first time in this volume. Written in 1919.

THE PASSING OF LOUIS (V. Starrett) — Written for this volume, October 1919, and here first printed.

ADVENTURING WITH R. L. S. (E. Feuerlicht) — Appears here for the first time in print.

To R. L. S. (A. Austin) — From *A Tale of True Love and Other Poems*, 1902.

THE BURIAL OF ROBERT LOUIS STEVENSON AT SAMOA (F. E. Coates) — From *The Book-Lover*, November-December, 1902.

ON A PORTRAIT OF "R. L. S." THE INVALID (A. Stringer) — From *The Bookman*, June, 1903.

To STEVENSON (C. Keeler) — From the *Impressions Quarterly*, December, 1904.

TUSITALA: TELLER OF TALES (M. H. Krout) — From *The Reader's Magazine*, September, 1905.

R. L. S. (A Johnstone) — From *Recollections of Robert Louis Stevenson in the Pacific*, Chatto & Windus, London, 1905.

STEVENSON (G. E. Montgomery) — From *The Pall Mall Magazine*, February, 1908.

ROBERT LOUIS STEVENSON (L. W. Reese) — From *The Mosher Books*, a catalogue, 1908; reprinted in *A Quiet Road*, Mosher, 1916.

THOUGHT OF STEVENSON (A. Upson) — From *The Bibelot*, March, 1909.

LEGEND OF PORTSMOUTH SQUARE (W. O. McGeeham) — Read at the Stevenson Fellowship Banquet in San Francisco, November 13, 1909. From *Robert Louis Stevenson in California*, by Katharine D. Osbourne, 1911.

TOASTS IN A LIBRARY (?) — From *The Mosher Books*, a catalogue, 1909. The reference to Stevenson begins with the last line of the penultimate stanza and continues to the end.

R. L. S. (E. Gosse) — From *Collected Poems*, 1911. Written some years before, in all probability.

PARAPHRASE: TO TRAVEL HOPEFULLY, etc. (F. Smith) — Written in 1910, and printed here for the first time.

R. L. S., ON READING *Travels With a Donkey* (F. Smith) — Written about 1910. Printed here for the first time.

"TREASURE ISLAND" (B. L. Taylor) — First printed in *The Chicago Tribune*; reprinted in *A Line-o'-Verse or Two*, 1911.

TREASURE ISLAND (P. Chalmers) — First printed in *Punch* (London); reprinted in *Littell's Living Age*, Aug. 5, 1911. Collected in *Green Days and Blue Days*, 1914.

THE OLD VAQUERO REMEMBERS ROBERT LOUIS STEVENSON (R. Rogers) — From *Lyrics, Songs and Idylls*, 1912.

AT THE ROBERT LOUIS STEVENSON FOUNTAIN (J. N. Hilliard) — From *Sunset*, November, 1912.

Anstruther Harbor. The stone was placed on the west front of Cunzie House, or, as Stevenson wrote it, 'Kenzie House,' by Miss Lorimer, Kellie Castle, and a few friends."

STEVENSON OF THE LETTERS (B. P. Neuman) — From *The Spectator*, January 27, 1900; reprinted in *Littell's Living Age*, March 17, 1900. In Hammerton.

"TUSITALA" (P. T. M.) — From *The Book Buyer*, February, 1900, where it appeared with the following note: "A subscriber writes that she has read Mr. Low's review of *Stevenson's Letters* with so much pleasure that she wishes every reader of *The Book Buyer* to see a poem which she has clipped from 'a daily paper' — she gives no more definite credit."

To STEVENSON (G. W. Hazard) — From *The Independent*, August 16, 1900. Miss Hazard is now well known as Grace Hazard Conkling.

A TOAST TO TUSITALA (B. Carman) — From *Reedy's Mirror*, November, 1900.

To ROBERT LOUIS STEVENSON (R. Burton) — From *The Century Magazine*, December, 1900.

STEVENSON'S BIRTHDAY (K. Miller) — From *An American Anthology*, edited by Edmund Clarence Stedman, 1900, where it appears without date or publication credit. The poem is based on an actual occurrence in the early life of Adelaide Ide; Stevenson's letter to the young person, who was born on February 29, is famous. The author of the poem is Katherine (Wise) Miller, daughter of Com. Henry A. Wise, U.S.N., and wife of Com. J. W. Miller, U.S.N.R. She was born at Spezia, Italy, 18—.

R. L. S. IN MEMORIAM (A. Dobson) — Dedication of the New Century Number of *The Student*, issued by the Students' Representative Council, University of Edinburgh, January, 1901. Reprinted in *Littell's Living Age*, May 25, 1901. Collected in *Carmina Votiva and Other Occasional Verses*, printed for private circulation, 1901. In Hammerton, and probably elsewhere.

R. L. STEVENSON (C. P. Nettleton) — From *The Book-Lover*, March-April, 1901.

STEVENSON-NICHOLSON (C. de Fornaro) — From *The Critic* (N. Y.), June, 1901, where it appears with a caricature of Stevenson, "á la Nicholson," by C. de Fornaro, who may have and probably did write the verses.

AT THE STEVENSON FOUNTAIN (W. Irwin) — From The Rubric, July, 1901.

To R. L. S. (C. W. Collins) — From *The Book Buyer, December*, 1901.

and Day; reprinted in *By the Aurelian Wall and Other Elegies*, 1898. In *Ballads and Lyrics*, London, 1902.

ON BEING ASKED FOR A SONG (R. W. Gilder) — From *The Poems of Richard Watson Gilder*, 1908. Probably sent to Isobel O. Strong, as indicated, about 1895.

IN MEMORIAM, R. L. STEVENSON (M. Armour) — From *The Home and Early Haunts of Robert Louis Stevenson*, W. H. White & Co., Edinburgh, 1895. The quoted lines used by the author as a text, are the last two lines of Stevenson's "Home no more home to me," first printed in 1889 and collected in *Songs of Travel*, 1896.

AT THE ROAD-HOUSE (B. Carman) — From *More Songs From Vagabondia*, 1895.

ROBERT LOUIS STEVENSON (F. Smith) — From *A Chest of Viols*, 1896, privately printed by Sherrat and Hughes, Manchester, England. Mr. Smith was an English gentleman of means, a resident of Manchester, and the owner of a famous collection of old violins. He died, I am informed, "three or four years ago."

ON A YOUTHFUL PORTRAIT OF ROBERT LOUIS STEVENSON (J. W. Riley) — Written about September, 1897, and printed with the portrait described, in *Scribner's Magazine*, December, 1897. Collected in *Home Folks*, 1900. Also in *The Lockerbie Book*, 1911, and *Complete Works*, 1913. Hammerton reprints it, and uses the portrait described as a frontispiece to his volume.

THE WORD OF THE WATER (B. Carman) — Written in 1897. From *By the Aurelian Wall, and Other Elegies*, 1898. The Stevenson Fountain, a granite shaft surmounted by a bronze galleon, was unveiled in Portsmouth Square, San Francisco, October 17, 1897. On its front are the words, "To Remember Robert Louis Stevenson," and a passage from Stevenson's *Christmas Sermon*.

THE LAST PORTRAIT IN STEVENSON'S GALLERY (?) — First printed in *The St. James Gazette* (London); reprinted in *McClure's Magazine*, January, 1898.

THE ROBERT LOUIS STEVENSON MEMORIAL IN PORTSMOUTH SQUARE (F. W. Carpenter) — From *Verses From Many Lands*, Paul Elder & Co., San Francisco, no date.

ROBERT LOUIS STEVENSON (E. Carleton) — From *The Chap-Book*, February 15, 1898.

(INSCRIPTION) — From *The Criterion*, October 21, 1899, where it is credited to *The Irish Independent*. The note states that the inscription is on a memorial stone that "has been placed to mark the lodging in which Stevenson lived at Anstruther Fife, while assistant engineer at

FOR R. L. S. ON VAEA TOP (L. I. Guiney) — First printed in *Robert Louis Stevenson*, etc. See above.

IN MEMORIAM STEVENSON (O. Wister) — From *The Atlantic Monthly*, April, 1895. In Hammerton.

TO ROBERT LOUIS STEVENSON (B. Porter) — From *The Lark*, June, 1895. In Hammerton.

A GRAVE IN SAMOA (J. Macfarlane) — Where this was first printed does not appear. I take it from *Every Day in the Year*, edited by James L. and Mary K. Ford, 1914, where the poem stands without date or publication credit. An artist signing himself J. Macfarlane illustrated an article on the Samoan Islands in *Harper's Magazine* for September, 1897, and possibly he is the author of our poem.

TO ROBERT LOUIS STEVENSON (H. K. Viele) — From *Every Day in the Year*; see above.

A SAMOAN LAMENT (Native) — I do not know what the title of this song may be, or whether it has a title. Isobel Osbourne Strong, in the *Century Magazine*, November, 1895, says: "There are many songs about Tusitala, as Mr. Stevenson was called in the islands — rousing boat songs, when the paddles all beat time, and the handles are clicked against the sides of the canoe to the rhythm of his name. . . In rowing Mr. Stevenson out to meet a passenger ship I have heard the boatmen keep time to '*Tusitala ma Aolele*' (Aolele is Mrs. Stevenson's native name, meaning "Beautiful as a flying cloud"). . . Then there are the dancing songs about Mr. Stevenson, depicting life at Vailima, which might be called topical, as they generally touched upon the small incidents of plantation life. These were composed by some servant or workman on the place. . . Other songs are long chants, with innumerable verses descriptive of Tusitala's wisdom, his house, his friendship for the natives, and his love for Samoa. One of those may be called the 'Song of the Roof-Iron,' or 'The Meeting of Tusitala and the Men of Vaie'e.' . . . The most beautiful of the songs are those that were composed in memory of Mr. Stevenson, and sung at Vailima after his death. One, referring to the steadfast loyalty of Mr. Stevenson to the High Chief of Mataafa, through peace and war, victory and defeat, has for its refrain:

> *Once Tusitala's friend,*
> *Always Tusitala's friend.*

Another describes a Samoan searching among the white people for one as good and kind as Tusitala." The song given here is the only one reproduced in a full English translation by Mrs. Strong — and possibly this is incomplete.

A SEAMARK (B. Carman) — Published separately in 1895, by Copeland

ROBERT LOUIS STEVENSON (R. Garnett) — From *The Illustrated London News*, December 22, 1894; reprinted in *The Critic* (N. Y.), Vol. 26. It was reprinted and altered in *The Queen and Other Poems*, 1901. The present version is the revised one. The original version, which appears in Hammerton, is as follows:

> *Wondrous as though a star with twofold light*
> *Should fill her lamp for either hemisphere,*
> *Piercing cold skies with scintillation clear,*
> *And glowing on the sultry southern night;*
> *Was miracle of him who could unite*
> *Pine and the purple harbour of the deer*
> *With palm-plumed islets that sequestered hear*
> *The far-off wave their zoning coral smite.*
>
> *Still roars the surf, still bounds the wave, but where*
> *Is one to see, and hear, and tell again?*
> *As dancers pause on an arrested air*
> *Fail the fast-thronging figures of the brain;*
> *And shapes unshapely huddle in dim lair,*
> *Awaiting ripe vitality in vain.*

ROBERT LOUIS STEVENSON: AN ELEGY (R. LeGallienne) — First printed in *The Daily Chronicle* (London), December 25, 1894; reprinted in *The Birmingham Gazette*, December 26, 1894, and probably in other journals. Collected in *Robert Louis Stevenson: An Elegy, and Other Poems Mainly Personal*, 1895.

SCOTLAND'S LAMENT (J. M. Barrie) — From *The Bookman*, January, 1895; reprinted in *McClure's Magazine*, February, 1895.

HOME FROM THE HILL (W. R. Nicoll) — From *Blackwood's Magazine*, February, 1895. The "text" is from Stevenson's famous "Requiem." In Hammerton.

I. M., R. L. S. (W. E. Henley) — Dated "February 1891" in all editions of Henley's poems that I have seen. Did Henley write his memorial in advance of the subject's death? Or was it written originally for another occasion? I find no specific mention of the poem in any of the books I have consulted. From *Poems*, 1898.

R. L. S., IN MEMORIAM (A. C. R.) — The date of this sonnet does not appear. It may have been first printed in Japp's *Robert Louis Stevenson* (1905), from which it is here taken; but obviously it was written shortly after Stevenson's death.

VALEDICTION (L. I. Guiney) — First printed in *The Century Magazine*, March, 1895. Reprinted in *Robert Louis Stevenson: A Study by A. B., with a Prelude and a Postlude by L. I. G.*, issued for private distribution by Copeland and Day, in May, 1895, in an edition of 250 copies. A. B. was Alice Brown.

known about 1897, although a few word changes have been made since. It has been reprinted many times; once, in 1901, by *The Rubric*, Chicago, with illustrations by J. C. Johansen. In 1914, the poem, the story of its adventures, and much delightful gossip of its author, appeared in a privately printed brochure, now extremely rare, written and published by Champion I. Hitchcock. The inception of "The Dead Men's Song," as it also has been called, was Allison's desire to round out to a satisfactory conclusion the four lines introduced by Stevenson into *Treasure Island*. The fifth verse usually is set in italics, as intended by the author, as a delicate intimation that the theme of a woman was foreign to the main idea, which he attempted to carry out as he believed Stevenson might have done. The present version contains its author's final revisions.

A BALLAD OF JOHN SILVER (J. Masefield) — From *Salt Water Ballads*, first published 1892-3; reprinted with additions, 1913.

TO PROSPERO IN SAMOA (Y. Y.) — From *The Bookman*, May, 1892. In Hammerton.

TO ROBERT LOUIS STEVENSFN (A. Lang) — Dedication of *The Secret Commonwealth of Elves, Fauns, and Fairies*, by Robert Kirk, edited by Lang, London, 1893. Collected in *Ban and Arrière Ban*, 1894.

BALLANT O' BALLANTRAE (A. Lang) — From *Ban and Arrière Ban*, 1894. Probably written some little time previous to this publication. It is likely that Stevenson saw it in manuscript.

WRITTEN IN A COPY OF MR. STEVENSON'S "CATRIONA" (W. Watson) — From *Odes and Other Poems*, 1894. Possibly earlier than this date would suggest; "Catriona" was published in 1893. In Hammerton.

TO TUSITALA IN VAILIMA (E. Gosse) — This poem, dated "September 1894" by its author, reached Stevenson at Vailima three days before his death. It was the last piece of poetry read by him, and was the subject of the last letter he wrote on the last day of his life. The verses were read by Lloyd Osbourne at the funeral. First printed in *In Russet and Green*, 1894, of which volume it was the dedication; reprinted in Hammerton, and elsewhere.

GREETING (F. J. Cox) — First printed in *The Weekly Sun* (evidently a London journal), November 11, 1894. The poem was sent by its author to Stevenson, at Vailima, but R. L. S. died before it could reach him. Reprinted in Japp's *Robert Louis Stevenson: a Record, an Estimate, and a Memorial*, 1905.

R. L. S. (A. E. Housman) — From *The Academy*, December 22, 1894.

ROBERT LOUIS STEVENSON (J. Davidson) — From *The Illustrated London News*, December 22, 1894; reprinted in *The Critic* (N. Y.), Vol. 26.

NOTES

More or less reference is made hereinafter to "Hammerton." The book referred to is *Stevensoniana*, edited by J. A. Hammerton, London, 1903; revised and enlarged edition, Edinburgh, 1910 — a mine of information for Stevenson enthusiasts.

APPARITION (W. E. Henley) — This well-known sonnet commemorates Stevenson's first visit to Henley, "in hospital," in February, 1875. It has been reprinted *ad nauseam*, since its first appearance in print, in *A Book of Verses*, 1888.

"KIDNAPPED" (?) — From *Punch* (London), August 7, 1886. This appreciative jingle was one of a series of rhymed book reviews appearing weekly in *Punch* at that time. The general title of the department was "Paper-Knife Poems," with the additional line, "By Our Special Book-Marker."

TO ROBERT LOUIS STEVENSON (R. B. Wilson) — From *The Critic* (N. Y.), September 17, 1887. In Hammerton.

TO ROBERT LOUIS STEVENSON ON HIS FIRST VISIT TO AMERICA (J. W. Riley) — Dated by its author "September 1887"; printed in the *New York World*, December 11, 1887. First collected in *Home Folks*, 1900; also in *The Lockerbie Book*, 1911, and *Complete Works*, 1913. In a note to this poem, in the latter, the editor, Edmund H. Eitel, Riley's nephew and biographer, says: "Mr. Riley found Stevenson's works particularly congenial reading."

TO R. L. S. (W. E. Henley) — From *A Book of Verses*, 1888. It will be noted that, despite its "memorial" tone, this poem was written in Stevenson's lifetime. R. L. S. died in 1894.

STEVENSON'S "UNDERWOODS" (E. M. Thomas) — From *The Century Magazine*, April, 1888.

DERELICT (Y. E. Allison) — Three stanzas of this vigorous chanty were written in 1891, and set to music by Henry Waller. The piece then was entitled "A Piratical Ballad"; it was published by Wm. A. Pond & Co., N. Y. Over the next six years, Mr. Allison revised and corrected and added, at various times, and the song was completed as now generally

Monahan, New Canaan, Conn., for his poem, "The Travellers"; to Small, Maynard & Co., Boston, and Bliss Carman, for the latter's poems, "A Seamark," "At the Road House," "A Toast to Tusitala," and "The Word of the Water"; to *The Bookman*, for Mt. Stringer's "On a Portrait of 'R. L. S.' the Invalid"; to Thomas B. Mosher, Portland, Me., and the author, for Miss Reese's "Robert Louis Stevenson"; and to any and all writers and publishers whose productions have been here reprinted without express permission, begging that they will forgive the freedom for the sake of "R. L. S." While every effort has been made to secure permission to reprint, in all cases where by any chance such permission seemed requisite, or was possible to obtain, there may have been oversights. These will be gladly corrected, if pointed out, in any future edition of the book. Sarah N. Cleghorn's "Saint R. L. S." is reprinted, by permission of the publishers, from *Portraits and Protests*, Henry Holt and Company, New York; "Samoa and R. L. S." is reprinted from *Sea Dogs and Men at Arms*, by Jesse E. Middleton, by courtesy of G. P. Putnam's Sons; "To Robert Louis Stevenson," by Alfred Austin, copyright, 1902, is reprinted through the courtesy of Harper & Bros., New York. The "Ballad of John Silver" is reprinted by permission of the publishers, The Macmillan Company, from John Masefield's *Salt Water Poems and Ballads*.

In addition to the above acknowledgments, I wish especially to thank my friends, Dr. A. J. Marks of Toledo, O., and Mr. J. Christian Bay of Chicago, for invaluable assistance in bringing together the numerous Stevenson tributes herein contained, and Mrs. Luther S. Livingston of Cambridge, Mass., for a similar kindness.

It is the intention of the editor to continue to collect verse-tributes to Robert Louis Stevenson, looking toward an enlarged edition of this anthology at some future date. Poets, or persons having in their possession poems not included in the present volume, are invited to send additional items to Vincent Starrett, 5611 West Lake Street, Chicago, Ill.

ACKNOWLEDGMENTS

For permission to reproduce the poems in this volume, grateful acknowledgments are extended to Charles Scribner's Sons, New York, for permission to use Stevenson's poem, "Over the Sea to Skye;" to The Bobbs-Merrill Company, Indianapolis, for permission to use James Whitcomb Riley's "To Robert Louis Stevenson on His First Visit to America," and "On a Youthful Portrait of Robert Louis Stevenson," both copyrighted by that company; to *The Century Magazine*, for "Stevenson's 'Underwoods'," by Edith M. Thomas, and Dr. Burton's "Robert Louis Stevenson"; to Young E. Allison, Louisville, Ky., for permission to use his ballad, "Derelict"; to The John Lane Co., New York, for William Watson's "Written in a Copy of Mr. Stevenson's 'Catriona'," Edmund Gosse's "To Tusitala in Vailima," and "R. L. S.," John Davidson's "Robert Louis Stevenson," Dr. Garnett's sonnet of the same title, Mr. Le Gallienne's "Robert Louis Stevenson, An Elegy," and Mr. Dobson's "R. L. S., In Memoriam"; to Owen Wister, Philadelphia, for his poem, "In Memoriam Stevenson"; to Houghton, Mifflin Company, Boston, for Richard Watson Gilder's "On Being Asked For a Song"; to Paul Elder & Co., San Francisco, for Mr. Carpenter's "The Robert Louis Stevenson Memorial"; to *The Independent*, for Mrs. Conkling's "To Stevenson"; to Bert Leston Taylor, Chicago, for his poem, "Treasure Island"; to *Sunset Magazine*, for Mr. Hilliard's "At the Robert Louis Stevenson Fountain"; to *The Overland Monthly*, for Mr. Greenwood's "To R. L. S."; to *The Book News Monthly*, for "Robert Louis Stevenson," by Ethel Talbot Scheffauer; to *Munsey's Magazine*, for Mr. Chalmers's "Robert Louis Stevenson"; to the *New York Times*, for "The Death of Flint," and to Mr. Chalmers and Houghton, Mifflin Company for "Friend o' Mine"; to Michael

ADVENTURING WITH R. L. S.

Treasure Island — dim and dark
In the dim blue distance — hark,
A call! And see — a sail!
Pirates? Nay, too fragile-pale
The dear captain of our bark.

Pale, yet smiling — Come, embark!
There, beyond those poplars stark,
Beckons, past the gleaming trail,
    Treasure Island!

What care we for hall and park,
Castled splendors, cities? — Mark,
How like silver-shimmering mail
Stir the poplars — like a veil
Lift the dimness and the dark —
    Treasure Island!
        — ETHEL FEUERLICHT

But vagabond Borrow uprose full proud
   And trolled a song of the road, I guess.
No doubt the chorus was somewhat loud —
   There was none to cavil, and many to bless.
And Stevenson's eyes were bright with tears,
For this was the judgment of his peers.

I like to think of that lusty crew
   Rollicking there like happy boys;
Singing the songs that gay dogs do,
   Scaring the Landlord with their noise —
And Master Will, with a hearty smack,
Slapping Louis upon the back.

And somewhere, too, in the haze of smoke,
   A little fellow, with eyes alert,
Chuckles, as at a gorgeous joke,
   And weeps a little, as if it hurt. . .
With a smile and a tear waits Alan Breck
To hang an arm on his master's neck.

                        — VINCENT STARRETT

THE PASSING OF LOUIS

He didn't wait for his laurel wreath;
    He didn't stay for the long applause.
Someone called from a distant heath,
    And he slipped away from the House of Shaws. . .
I think they met him along the road,
And led the way to his new abode.

Perhaps a group of the roving kin,
    Smiling a welcome, strangely sweet,
Were waiting there when the ship came in,
    And cheered, and hoisted him off his feet.
Perhaps they carried him shoulder-high
Who had journeyed "over the sea to Skye."

Somewhere along the highway then,
    The rest would tarry until he came —
At the Friendly Inn of the Joyous Men,
    With its ringing glasses and hearth aflame.
Yes, that was it! It was just that way:
I think I must have been there, that day.

Ah, what a racket there must have been
    When *he* pushed open the swinging doors;
What a burst of jovial, boisterous din,
    With steins on tables and heels on floors
Beating and kicking away like mad! —
That was a way those fellows had.

And there they sat who had gone before:
    Sir Walter loomed at the head, I think;
And Fielding's thunder and Jonson's roar
    Probably made the goblets clink.
The Reverend Laurence may have smiled,
But I fancy his eyes were a trifle wild. . .

A HOUSE IN SARANAC

There stands a house in Saranac
   Beside a shady way,
That knew the tread of Stevenson
   In his little day,

And down its friendly corridors
   That gave him joy to see,
The ready laugh of Stevenson
   Sounded merrily.

Though now his lonely bed is made
   Upon a far-off hill,
The memory of Stevenson
   Dwells in it still;

And so because He loved the man
   Who roses gleaned from rue,
God guards the house of Stevenson
   The long years through.
      — GEORGE STEELE SEYMOUR

Enters he like a prince, of right
   (Not one to palter or to sue he!)
And all my best of love I lay
   ˙ At the feet of Robert Louis.

Dashing and free and picturesque,
   No wind of time has chilled him yet:
In art our darling mousquetaire —
   Romance and a cigarette!
       .   .   .   .

After such guests who shall have leave
   To win our grace with song and story? —
Yes, one that now belated comes,
   With no small meed of glory.

Richard! I would be young to-night:
   Your philter quick! — without demur he
Begins the spell, while magic airs
   Blow to us out of Surrey.

I join with him th' eternal chase
   Thro' peopled ways and sylvan places,
While Beauty ever flies before —
   Yet oft looks back with luring graces.

Ah! seeker of the Golden Girl,
   What pranks you played me in that dream! —
Methought a fortune fair was mine
   At the Inn of the Singing Stream.
                  — MICHAEL MONAHAN

THE TRAVELLERS

Favored am I with guests of fame
   Who pass not with the passing year,
But still return to the ingle's glow
   Or the lamp's embracing cheer.

And first of these the jester quaint,
   Old Shandy of the Satyr smile
And dropping tear that pardon claims
   For his page of honeyed guile.

The good man craves an hour of ease
   To spin the tale that lives for aye;
Tho' I mislike the parson's leer,
   To Trim and Toby who'll say nay?

Now Yorick fades, and comes a knock
   That sets my pulses beating wild,
For lo! there stands within the door
   The Muses' unforgotten child.

Ah, Heine! haste not on your way,
   Strange wreaths of pain the Gods intend you:
Unwounded yet by Love and Fame,
   Stay, while the golden years befriend you!

He weaves his weird of song and speech
   That thrills the list'ning soul with wonder;
Then swift departs — as tho' he heard
   On Brocken's height the thunder.

Deepens the night. I trim the lamp
   That often burns till dawning gray;
When sudden from the outer dark
   There rings a challenge bold and gay.

SAMOA AND R. L. S.

What if the bones of Stevenson
   (As in the sight of an ancient Seer)
Gathered themselves, and soon had won
   Flesh and muscle and tailors' gear!
What if Stevenson, thus arisen,
   Out of the glooms of death came back,
Finding Samoa his German prison
   Rapturous under the Union Jack!

Wouldn't he hold his honest head
   High and proud in the golden days?
Wouldn't he love the man who said,
   "Here is the flag and here it stays!"
Wouldn't he write a wonderful tale
   Celebrating the sudden fight
After the Anzac's headlong sail?
   Stevenson — who is dead to-night.

       — JESSE EDGAR MIDDLETON

ON CERTAIN CRITICS OF STEVENSON

They call him "little master," parrot-wise,
  And praise his "style" with patronizing air;
  Find evidence of genius, "here and there" —
The smug, damned critics with their alibis.
Glutting the journals with their hackneyed drone;
  Like moths attracted to the candle's flame,
  Seeking reflected lustre from his name
They impudently write below, their own.
Standing beneath a sprig of mistletoe,
  Self-hung, and subtly labeled "R. L. S."
  They smirk, and coyly wait the blind caress
Of Tribute's indiscriminate overflow. . .
  But the great master, from his thronging shrine,
  Reveals no favour, manifests no sign.

— Vincent Starrett

SAINT R. L. S.

Sultry and brazen was the August day
   When Sister Stanislaus went down to see
   The little boy with the tuberculous knee.

And as she thought to find him, so he lay:
   Still staring, through the dizzy waves of heat,
   At the tall tenement across the street.

But did he see the dreary picture? Nay!
   In his mind's eye a sunlit harbor showed,
   Where a tall pirate ship at anchor rode.

Yes, he was full ten thousand miles away!
   The Sister, when she turned his pillow over,
   Kissed "Treasure Island" on its well-worn cover.

                      — SARAH N. CLEGHORN

ROBERT LOUIS STEVENSON

Out of the land of the ancient bards
    A wandering minstrel strayed;
Courage and hope were the song he sang,
    And faith was the string he played.
"I care not what the end," he cried,
    "So the road be fair and free;
For the greater gift of life is his
    Who travels cheerily!"

Earth was his house and heaven his roof;
    Sun, moon, and stars his light;
Voices of wind and wood and wave
    His music day and night.
Over his clouds the lark sang still;
    And when the light was gone,
Thrilling the dark of crouching doom,
    His nightingale sang on.

So let us be, as the minstrel sang,
    Of faith, and hope, and love,
Though the snarling waters scowl beneath,
    And thunder rolls above.
After the rain, the night of stars;
    After the night, the dawn;
And that day goes down to a splendid death,
    Which lights another's morn!

— STEPHEN CHALMERS

We was feared he would open his jaw,
  An' sit up an' yell: "Flint dead? To Hell!
  Fetch aft the rum, M'Graw!"

But come! Are ye scared? He's a grinnin' stiff,
  Deep-buried Savannah way.
Will ye show yer starn to a boozy ghost,
  When Flint don't walk — by day.
I saw him dead wi' these 'ere headlights,
  I shovelled in some o' the sod.
It was these 'ere hands as closed his eyes —
  Though they wouldn't stay shut, b' God!

But we weighted 'em down with gold doubloons
  (He'd always an eye for gold);
An' we tied up his jaw with an old, red sash,
  When sartain sure he was cold;
While the green parrot squawked around his face,
  An' pecked at his cold, blue lips,
Cryin', "Pieces of eight!" But Flint was gone
  To beat up phantom ships!

— STEPHEN CHALMERS

THE DEATH OF FLINT

(Said the fellow with the bandage: ". . . Dear heart, but he died bad, did Flint." — TREASURE ISLAND.)

Of the seven that day as sailed away
    To bury the pirate's hoard,
With a godless grin on his blue-black chin
    Just Flint returned aboard.
His cock-eye twitched and luffed askew
    As he croaked by the cabin door:
"'T will go under the sod with me, b' God!
    Then I'll beat up Hell for more!"

Oh, well I remember how hard he died,
    That night on Savannah coast;
How he shot three men and took Billy Bones
    For an honest trader's ghost.
We darsn't go near, but we heard him sing,
    An' the bottles go smash and crash,
As he fought wi' the devils as clung to his throat,
    An' cursed 'em for lubber trash!

He fought an' he fumed, an' he cursed an' he swore,
    An' raved o'er his buried pile,
Singin', *"Fifteen men on the dead man's chest,"*
    An' a-soakin' up rum the while.
An' he yo-ho-ho'd, an' he stabbed the air,
    An' he strangled the tangled bed,
An' he cracked the wall wi' a blow o' his fist,
    An' laughed — *his* laugh — and was dead!

He was blue wi' the rum that had fouled his hawse —
    (Oh, an ugly devil was Flint!)
We could hardly believe as he'd come to port,
    For his eye had the same old squint.
When we laid him out snug in the hole we dug,

Ay, we were boys together — comrades still
 In the glamorous hours of dusk that (you know!) lend
Fine dreams to finer fellows — There's my hand,
 Mine own, familiar friend!

— Stephen Chalmers

FRIEND O' MINE

When first I met you, you were dead, while I
   Had scarce begun to live. And where we met
Was on some far-blown island where the shores
   Upon an opal sea, reef-clutched, were set.

You were a man while I was yet a boy;
   But, friend o' mine, were we not boys together?
Had we not jeered the gales at Stornaway
   And made the Sound o' Mull in stormy weather?

Did we not watch the seagull dare the foam,
   Dip to the wave, fleck it and scream its scorn?
Did we not say: "There goes a sailor's wraith!
   Where was he drowned? I'll wager off the Horn."

In boyish dreams did we not often view
   The sea-hewn cave as where a baresark leered —
Long-haired and gaunt and foaming at the mouth,
   Grinding his teeth till blood ran down his beard?

Did we not tread the snowbound wilderness,
   Bearing in turn our common sorrow's pack?
Did we not hear the grinding mills of God
   And make that bitter camp by Saranac?

Did we not watch the South Sea palms at dusk?
   By morn, at sea, the flying-fish at play?
Did we not swear again that we were friends
   As from our sheering copper burst the spray?

And had we not a circle of strange friends,—
   Rough seasman, polished prince and tattered tramp?
Ah, in those days what stirring tales were passed
   By galley fire, peat hearth and gypsy camp!

TO ROBERT LOUIS STEVENSON

How often have I sat beneath thy spell,
O Sorcerer, who feared nor death nor hell!
But, like thine own bird "singing in the rain,"
Thy voice comes true and clear above thy pain.
O wanderer, whose lips made no complaint!
Brave exile, fighting on, though weak and faint;
No notes of coward fear you ever sang;
Your tones with vibrant hope and courage rang.
And we, who read thy messages today,
Gather fresh strength to pass upon our way.
Sleep on, sweet soul, beneath the Southern Cross;
Ours is the gain, Samoa's is the loss!

— Edwin Carlile Litsey

ROBERT LOUIS STEVENSON

He sings for youth, the passionate and sad,
   Youth that despairs and triumphs and is blind;
And ever through the singing, clean and glad,
   The keen cool moorland runs, and the north wind.

A starkness and a fierceness and a pride
   That still defies the night, and with caught breath
Cries hope — tho louder, not to be denied,
   The sullen trumpets of the court of death

Peal through the page with strong, insistent surge
   And ever is the blackness tenanted:
Somewhere far off, a song rings like a dirge,
   And a veiled King stands by the poet's head.

            — Ethel Talbot Scheffauer

TO R. L. S.

A wandering singer through the realm of dreams,
  He tuned his pipe to Life's brief-voicéd song,
And danced adown a pathway lit with gleams
  Of fortitude and resignation born.
No comrade spirit knew his staunch heart's pain
  Nor saw his footsteps lag, nor heard a sigh —
We only knew a sweetness naught could maim,
  As hand in hand with Courage he passed by.
He breathed upon life's truths with magic, rare,
  Until they took the beauty from his soul,
Or wrought fact into romance — Oh, so fair!
  With artistry beyond the common goal.
    So with blessed labor, finding Life's face grey,
    He smiled, and charmed the haunting hours away.

                — R. R. GREENWOOD

LONG JOHN SILVER

There is no rhyme for you, John, poets say —
 No rhyme for Silver, queer as that may be;
 And yet, for that you've been so much to me,
I'll put you in a sonnet, anyway.
Ah, what a scoundrel were you in that day
 When buccaneer and pirate sailed the sea!
 Your hand was ever on your snickersnee,
Itching to meet somebody it might slay. . .

Whimsical villain! Winsome mutineer!
 Although you've caused my hair to stand erect,
 While reading of your devil's doings when
You taught Jim Hawkins what a thing was Fear,
 I love you. . . But may all good saints protect
 Me from the wiles of wooden-legged men!

— Vincent Starrett

This ground whereon the fountain plays
  Shall sacred be against the years,
Shall hallowed be — since he has passed
  To the Valhalla of his peers.

And here shall be nor East nor West;
  For all the trails shall blend as one,
And men shall come from all the world
  To drink to Louis Stevenson.

— John Northern Hilliard

AT THE ROBERT LOUIS STEVENSON FOUNTAIN

    He was a princely vagabond,
        A restless rover from his birth,
    An alien lodger for the night
        In this old wayside inn of earth.

    A simple-hearted wayfarer,
        With spring and summer in his breast,
    A comrade of the roving foot,
        And fevered of the great unrest,

    Who now hath fared on trails beyond
        The range marked by the cobalt rim
    Of sordid things — beyond the pale
        Of horizons forever dim —

    A nomad, safe at last within
        The world-old harbor gates of time,
    The master, whose blithe feet once strayed
        Among the hills of prose and rhyme.

    To think that once upon a time,
        In ragged luck, he passed this way,
    That his eyes, too, once followed far
        The scudding sails across the Bay;

    That he, too, saw the plume of smoke
        That marks the outbound steamer's trail,
    That he, too, heard the winches creak,
        And saw the cargoes, bale on bale,

    Fed to the yawning maws of ships —
        The coursers of the seven seas,
    That strain, like hounds, upon the leash,
        Impatient to be down the breeze.

THE OLD VAQUERO REMEMBERS ROBERT LOUIS STEVENSON

Though I live to the age of eagles,
And the winds shall blow through me like a net,
One day from the rest I shall not forget
Though I live to the age of eagles,
But remember, and guard more than treasures of gold;
Though the winds shall blow through me like a net,
And I am shaken by wind and cold.
— REGINALD ROGERS

TREASURE ISLAND

A lover breeze to the roses pleaded,
    Failed and faltered, took heart and advanced;
Up over the beaches, unimpeded,
    A great Red Admiral ducked and danced;
But the boy with the book saw not, nor heeded,
    Reading entranced — entranced!

He read, nor knew that the brown bees bumbled;
    He woke no whit to the tea bell's touch,
The drowsy pigeons that wheeled and tumbled,
    (But how should a pirate reck of such?)
He read, and the flaming flower-beds crumbled
    At the tap of the sea-cook's crutch!

And lo, there leapt for him dolphins running
    The peacock seas of the buccaneer,
Lean, savage reefs where the seals lay sunning,
    The curve of canvas, the creak of gear;
For ever the Master's wondrous cunning
    Lent him of wizard lear!

  .   .   .   .

But lost are the flowerful days of leisure,
    Lost with their wide-eyed ten-year-old
Yet if you'd move to a bygone measure,
    Or shape your heart to an ancient mould,
Maroons and schooners and buried treasure
    Wrought on a page of gold —

Then take the book in the dingy binding:
    Still the shadows come, bearded, great;
And swaggering files of sea-thieves winding
    Back, with their ruffling cut-throat gait,
Reclaim an hour when we first went finding
    Pieces of Eight — of Eight!

                      — PATRICK CHALMERS

"TREASURE ISLAND"

Comes little lady, a book in hand,
A light in her eyes that I understand,
And her cheeks aglow from the faery breeze
That sweeps across the uncharted seas.
She gives me the book, and her word of praise
A ton of critical thought outweighs:
"I've finished it, Daddie!" — a sigh thereat.
"Are there any more books in the world like that?"

No, little lady, I grieve to say
That of all the books in the world today
There's not another that's quite the same
As this magic book with the magic name.
Volumes there be that are pure delight,
Ancient and yellowed or new and bright;
But — little and thin, or big and fat —
There are no more books in the world like that.

And what, little lady, would I not give
For the wonderful world in which you live!
What have I gathered one-half as true
As the tales Titania whispers you?
Ah, late we learn that the only truth
Was that which we found in the Book of Youth.
Profitless others, and stale, and flat; —
There are no more books in the world like that.

— BERT LESTON TAYLOR

R. L. S.

ON READING "TRAVELS WITH A DONKEY IN THE CEVENNES"

How sweet the ways when we poor mortals stray
   When, with enlightened eyes unveiled we see
   Earth's wondrous beauty and her mystery!
Nature revealed, a living thing alway,
Alert in listening night or bountiful day,
   Moves to our mood with finest sympathy,
   With watchful service sets our spirits free,
Sings in our joy or weeps our tears away.

Surely the fault is ours, so long we rest
   Content with darkened vision at the gate,
When we might stand within, in reverence drest,
   With sense refined, with subtle joy elate,
   In that hushed portal where such wonders wait
As they may see whom God hath fitly blest!

— FREDERIC SMITH

PARAPHRASE

To travel hopefully is a better thing than to arrive. — R. L. S.

Better the pilgrim's staff, the cheerful song,
The distant hills to beckon us along,
A free highway and the wide sky above,
The foot to travel and the heart to love,
Youth's eager fancies and the morning light,
Than the high festival of crowning night.

So long our vision shines, our hopes befriend,
Better the journey than the journey's end.
The cozy resting place that shines ahead,
Is not so blessed as the step we tread.
Better a mountain streamlet in the sun,
Than the still pool with all our journeyings done.

Better the toil and stress, though spent in vain,
Than the brief joys we labour to obtain.
The flowers we stop to gather by the way
Before our journey's end are thrown away,
But all the joy of search and sight is ours,
That shall go with us tho' we lose the flowers.

Thrice happy he who learns the truth I tell,
He shall arrive at last, and all be well.

— FREDERIC SMITH

R. L. S.

Rest, oh thou restless angel, rest at last,
   High on thy mountain peak that caps the waves;
   Anguish no more thy delicate soul enslaves,
Dream-clouds no more thy slumber overcast.
Adventurous angel, fold thy wings! The vast
   Pacific forest, with its architraves,
   The stillness of its long liana'd naves,
Involves thee in a silence of times past.

Thou whom we loved, a child of sportive whim,
   So fair to play with, comfort, thrill or chide,
    Art grown as ancient as thine island gods,
As mystic as the menacing seraphim,
   As grim as priests upon a red hill-side,
    Or lictors shouldering high their sheaves of rods.

                      — EDMUND GOSSE

TOASTS IN A LIBRARY

I raise my glass (Carthusian brew,
   And pure the emerald shines),
A sip to thee, my Rabelais —
   The wisest of divines.

But lest thy genial earthly soul
   Should claim too much of me,
I turn to him who to the Lark
   Gave his own extacy.

A subtle drink and delicate
   One owes to Thomas Browne,
And noble port when Gibbon hands
   Sonorous wisdom down.

For thee, suave Horace, unperplexed,
   Well-bred, well-nourished man,
I would unstop an amphora
   Of thy Falernian.

I name them not (too great to name)
   The choice Hellenic Few,
I drink in silence piously:
   Then turn I, friend, to you.[1]

O, smiling soul, that craved the sun,
   Yet ample suffering bore,
This be your praise: "He loved art much,
   But men and nature more."

[1] R. L. S.

Drink and the devil had done with the rest,
Yo-ho-ho and a bottle of rum!''

Oh, the little bronze ship has returned to its place
To the stone by the poplar trees,
And the little bronze sails though they gleam in the sun
Will not answer the morning breeze.
Now the ghost song has died on the pale phantom lips,
And gone are the mast and the men,
And the little bronze ship is back safe from the trip
Till it goes on a cruise again.

There it lies through the day, till the noise dies away
And the moonshine is soft on the square:
Then its queer phantom crew take it out on the blue
And their chanty rings weird on the air:
"Fifteen men on a dead man's chest,
Yo-ho-ho and a bottle of rum!
Drink and the devil had done with the rest,
Yo-ho-ho and a bottle of rum.''

— W. O. McGeeham

LEGEND OF PORTSMOUTH SQUARE

Oh, the little bronze ship at the anchor chain tugs
And the light on the bright sails gleams,
In the moonshine and mist it is headed southwest
For a cruise on the sea of dreams.
All deserted the anchorage place in the square,
There are none who may look at it now;
With a brave off-shore wind that is warning behind
It is churning the foam with its prow.

With a queer phantom crew it is off on the blue,
And the blocks in the rigging ring,
When the wraith voices rise to the tropical skies
And this is the song that they sing:
"Fifteen men on a dead man's chest,
Yo-ho-ho and a bottle of rum!
Drink and the devil had done with the rest,
Yo-ho-ho and a bottle of rum!"

There is Morgan, and Merry, and savage Long John
With his crutch, on the little bronze ship,
And old Smollett, the Skipper, is shaking his head,
As he thinks of that other trip;
And the oracle parrot, the sage Captain Flint,
Still is chatt'ring of bloodshed and wreck.
With his big dreamy eyes staring up at the skies,
See, the master is pacing the deck.

There are doubloons and loot, there is battle to boot,
Ere they ever return to their port;
With a rhythmical swing now the crew's voices ring
In a song of a gruesome sort:
"Fifteen men on a dead man's chest,
Yo-ho-ho and a bottle of rum!

THOUGHT OF STEVENSON

High and alone I stood on Calton Hill
   Above the scene that was so dear to him,
   Whose exile dreams of it made exile dim.
October wooed the folded valleys till
In mist they blurred, even as our eyes upfill
   Under a too-sweet memory; spires did swim,
   And gables rust-red, on the grey sea's brim —
But on these heights the air was soft and still.

Yet not all still: an alien breeze will turn
   Here, as from bournes in aromatic seas,
As round old shrines a new-freed soul might yearn
   With incense of rich earthly reveries.
     Vanish the isles: Mist, exile, searching pain,
     But the brave soul is free, is home again!
                      — Arthur Upson

ROBERT LOUIS STEVENSON

In his old gusty garden of the North,
He heard lark-time the uplifting Voices call;
Smitten through with Voices was the evenfall —
At last they drove him forth.

Now there were two rang silverly and long;
And of Romance, that spirit of the sun,
And of Romance, spirit of youth, was one;
And one was that of Song.

Gold-belted sailors, bristling buccaneers,
The flashing soldier, and the high, slim dame,
These were the Shapes that all around him came,—
That we let go with tears.

His was the unstinted English of the Scot,
Clear, nimble, with the scriptural tang of Knox
Thrust through it like the far, strict scent of box,
To keep it unforgot.

No frugal Realist, but quick to laugh,
To see appealing things in all he knew,
He plucked the sun-sweet corn his fathers grew,
And would have naught of chaff.

David and Keats, and all good singing men,
Take to your hearts this Covenanter's son,
Gone in mid-years, leaving our years undone,
Where you do sing again!
— Lizette Woodworth Reese

R. L. S.

Within the circle of the Fabled Sea,
   Where golden galleons once ploughed their way,
   He dwelt in exile; here with Princely sway
He ruled a realm of brave Romance, which he
Begat with wizard pen. 'Twas not to be
   Again to roam his Scottish moorlands gray,
   Nor wear the garlands won till close of day;
Yet, to the end, he smiled at Fate's decree,
And, smiling, drew new magic from the West
   To charm the stranger's ear. Now memory hath
Communion aye with him where he was guest
   In many a star-girt Isle, until the path
     He trode, with manly patience yet with pain,
     Reminds us how his exile was our gain.

                — Arthur Johnstone

STEVENSON

His lyric soul like some sweet seraph came
  And burned with lustrous glamour for a while,
  Then pitifully paled and passed: the guile
Of crafty art could neither chill nor tame
His glad alluring fancy, and his name
  Hints of rare tales that bring the tear or smile,
  Wrought with the fluency of magic style
And with the splendour of the oriflame:
I read his books as one may read the skies
  That show protean forms and colours blent
    By some transfiguring and translating chance,
And then I seem to look on life with eyes
  Grown large and lucent, full of bland assent
    To all the wands and wonders of romance.

Whether upon some strange isle of the sea,
  Where eager daring seeks its treasure-trove,
  Or in some placid and umbrageous cove
Where ships lie safe when bitter winds blow free,
And where wild birds may whistle all their glee
  Through the cool shadows of a southern grove;
  Whether in deep gray glooms where phantoms rove,
And at some harsh intruding footstep flee,—
He guides us with the genius of the gnome,
  That laughs at common mortals who can know
    Nothing of fairy loves and subtle flights:
And thus we wander with him through the gloam
  Of haunted summers or where starshines flow
    Through spectral cloisters in Arabian nights.
        — GEORGE EDGAR MONTGOMERY

TUSITALA: TELLER OF TALES

Dweller in many lands, he sought the heights
   And laid him down to sleep
Under the stars that, through the tropic nights,
   Burn in the purple deep.

There the first splendors of the dawning day
   Break o'er the sea's blue rim;
There the last glories of the sunset stay,
   As though they shone for him.

The white surf, far below, leaps high in air,
   The winds the palm-trees shake,
The silvery rains sweep by — he is not there;
   They call: he will not wake.

— Mary H. Krout

TO STEVENSON

Wanderer o'er life's inhospitable seas,
   With galleon sails to waft thee unto lands
   Of old romance, where jocund fancy stands,
Luring sad hearts of youth, where tropic trees
Rustle before the trade-wind's welcome breeze,
   And warm blue waves roll up on coral strands,
   Or, on the reef, with clapping of white hands;
Teller of tales the world afar to please,
Thy caravel sailed forth o'er chartless waves,
   But ere it left, a mighty far-off cry
     Reached o'er the sea,— the tardy world's acclaim:
Hail and farewell to him who fearless braves
   The unresisting deep with spirit high,
     Bequeathing kindliness, more prized than fame.

                          CHARLES KEELER

ON A PORTRAIT OF "R. L. S." THE INVALID

Was't this poor dun, thin, sombre, tattered bird
   Once made so merry down Earth's every dale?
Not by his coat, then, but the songs we heard,
   Let us remember now the Nightingale!

                    — Arthur Stringer

THE BURIAL OF ROBERT LOUIS STEVENSON AT SAMOA

Where shall we lay you down to rest?
Where will you sleep the very best?
Mirthful and tender, dear and true —
Where shall we find a grave for you?

They thought of a spirit brave as light,
And they bore him up to a lonely height,
And they laid him there, where he loved to be,
On a mountain gazing o'er the sea.

They thought of a soul aflood with song,
And they buried him where, the summer long,
Myriad birds his requiem sing,
And the echoing woods about him ring.

They thought of a love that life redeems,
Of a heart the home of perfect dreams,
And they left him there, where the worlds aspire
In the sunrise glow and the sunset fire!

— FLORENCE EARLE COATES

TO R. L. S.

Written after reading, a second time, the posthumous fragment "Weir of Hermiston."

I never saw you, never grasped your hand,
   Nor wrote nor read lines absence loves to trace,
   Ne'er with you sate in your accustomed place,
Nor waited for your coming on sea or land.
But this I know, if along unseen strand,
   Or anywhere in God's eternal space,
   You heard my voice, or I beheld your face,
That we should greet and both would understand.

So, till that hour, wherever you abide,
   On circling star or interstellar sea,
   Or where, from man's imagination free,
There moves no planet and there sounds no tide,
Welcome, as though from friend long known and tried,
   This gift of loving fellowship from me.

— ALFRED AUSTIN

TO R. L. S.

Buried on the crest of Vaea Mountain, Samoa, December 4, 1894.

> Where the mist-spirits float their pennons gray
>   On Vaea's gusty mountain crest, is he
>   Keeping the bivouac of eternity
> Pavilioned like a god. Day after day
> He listens to the epic winds that stray
>   Vagrant around the world; and birds that flee
>   Across the vasty reaches of the sea
> Sing him the saga of their weary way.
>
> Teller of tales, dear, venturous, yearning heart,
> Magician, rest upon your peak, apart
>   From beaten paths and smoke and cities' towers,
> And dream new dreams, unbroken save only when
> The child-like, reverent, dark-skinned island men
>   Pant up the steep cliff, laden with tropic flowers.

— CHARLES W. COLLINS

AT THE STEVENSON FOUNTAIN

(OLD PORTSMOUTH SQUARE, SAN FRANCISCO)

Perhaps from out the thousands passing by —
   The city's hopeless lotos-eaters these,
   Blown from the four winds of the Seven Seas
For common want to common company —
Perhaps some one may lift a heavy eye
   And smile with freshening memories when he sees
   Those golden pennons bellying in the breeze
And spread for ports where fair adventures lie.
And oh, that such a one might stay a space
   And taste of sympathy till to his ears
Might come a tale of him who knew the grace
   To suffer sweetly through the bitter years,
To catch the smiles concealed in Fortune's face
   And draw contentment from a cup of tears!

— WALLACE IRWIN

STEVENSON-NICHOLSON

In winter I sat up all night
To think of grewsome things to write;
In summer, quite the other way,
I plucked some garden verse each day.

And does it not seem strange to you
That Nicholson this picture drew?
For though I'm dead, I am not half
So dead as dear old Beggarstaff.
— C. DE FORNARO

R. L. STEVENSON

With boyish shouts he cries out for the sea,
  With manhood's might he makes a clear-cut way,
  With womanly winning grace he lights the day,
And round his feet we cluster breathlessly.
— CHARLES P. NETTLETON

R. L. S.: IN MEMORIAM

These to his memory. May the age arriving,
    As ours recall
That bravest heart, that gay and gallant striving,
    That laurelled pall!

Blithe and rare spirit! We who later linger,
    By bleaker seas,
Sigh for the touch of the Magician's finger,
    His golden keys!

— Austin Dobson

STEVENSON'S BIRTHDAY

"How I should like a birthday!" said the child,
  "I have so few, and they so far apart."
She spoke to Stevenson — the Master smiled —
  "Mine is to-day; I would with all my heart
That it were yours; too many years have I!
Too swift they come, and all too swiftly fly."

So by a formal deed he there conveyed
  All right and title in his natal day,
  To have and hold, to sell or give away,—
Then signed, and gave it to the little maid.

Joyful, yet fearing to believe too much,
  She took the deed, but scarcely dared unfold.
Ah, liberal Genius! at whose potent touch
  All common things shine with transmuted gold!
A day of Stevenson's will prove to be
Not part of Time, but Immortality.
— Katherine Miller

TO ROBERT LOUIS STEVENSON

Dear ghost,— whose ruddy presence needs must fling
A ray of cheer among thy brother shades
In your pale land of Sleep,— thy legacy
The years make richer.
               For the fellowship
Of gallant souls who move down stirring ways
Of blithe adventure; for the moods of dream
That blossomed, at the conjuring call of Art,
Into Life's festal flowers of Romance;
For lyric interludes of Song, whose sound
Comes in pathetic cadences; for words
Apt, rare, and full of wisdom, touching deeps
On deeps of human passion: for such gifts
Surely the guerdon is love's long renown.

But most, O Comrade ours, we owe to thee
For that brave gospel thou didst ever bring —
Not pulpit-wise, but sweet as speech of birds:
Courage and kindliness and joy-of-life
Even in its motley and keen-edged with pain;
High spirit against evil, and the laugh
Unbitter; and that indomitable belief
In brotherhood. 'Twould shame us, looking on
Thy struggle and thy triumph, should we play
The craven; yea, thy present happy peace
Heartens all laggards.
                  Therefore seems it meet
To hail thee hero, fondly to recall
Thy valiant days, thy victory over doom,—
Child of delight and heir of loveliness,
Great friend, whose followers would fain be true.
                          — RICHARD BURTON

A TOAST TO TUSITALA

Eight men sat at the board,
From the West and the East they came;
And many and light were the toasts that night
Till someone named a name.

"To Robert Louis!" Then all
Stood up with a single mind;
And sober and brave was the toast they gave
The prince of the roving kind.

"Silent and standing!" Ay,
For the East and the West are one,
And the loving man has the world for his clan,
When all is said and done.
— BLISS CARMAN

TO STEVENSON

Free from my plodding mind,
　Hugging myself for glee,
Sometimes I ran with the wind,
　And sometimes he ran with me.
"Straight away from the start," called he,
　"We'll keep the pace together!"
He chuckled, whirling my soul away
　Into the shining weather.

Out in the silver air
　The laughter of waters rang:
The broad blue heaven was bare,
　The cheerful forest sang,
And in my heart upsprang
　Most blissful questioning — whether
Your soul ran with mine and the wind's
　Into the jolly weather?

Meseems I heard you say
　"'Tis the tune to travel to,
'Over the hills and far away,'
　With never an end in view."
Surely the wind and I and you
　Are vagabonds together,
On the road that leads both night and day
　Into the friendly weather.

— GRACE W. HAZARD

"TUSITALA"

(R. L. S.)

Teller of Tales from the passionless North,
   True mate of the manifold brotherhood,
Swept by the winds and the drift and the surge,
   Borne in on hearts that you understood,

Strong was your breath with the cry of the sea,
   Rife was your thought with the strife on the shore;
Quick was your maid with her love for her love,
   Skilful your hand in the craft of your lore.

We know the tale of the hot, choking blood,
   We see the shadow — the scroll on the wall;
We read the rhyme of the thorn in the rose,
   We greet the courage unflinching through all.

Stop't though your lips with the dust of our hills,
   Hark to the Wind-god astir on the wold;
"Talofa lee!"[1] and the crags answer back,
   "His spirit still lives in the tales that he told."
                      — P. T. M.

---

[1] *"Love to you Chief." A Samoan's greeting.*

STEVENSON OF THE LETTERS

Long, hatchet face, black hair, and haunting gaze,
   That follows, as you move about the room,
Ah! that is he who trod the darkening ways,
   And plucked the flowers upon the edge of doom.

The bright, sweet-scented flowers that star the road
   To death's dim dwelling, others heed them not,
With sad eyes fixed upon that drear abode,
   Weeping, and wailing their unhappy lot.

But he went laughing down the shadowed way,
   The boy's heart leaping still within his breast,
Weaving his garlands when his mood was gay,
   Mocking his sorrows with a solemn jest.

The high gods gave him wine to drink; a cup
   Of strong desire, of knowledge, and of pain;
He set it to his lips and drank it up
   Smiling, then turned unto his flowers again.

These are the flowers of that immortal strain,
   Which, when the hand that plucked them drops and dies,
Still keep their radiant beauty free from stain,
   And breathe their fragrance through the centuries.

                            — B. PAUL NEUMAN

(INSCRIPTION)

"Robert Louis Stevenson lived in this house in the summer of 1868.

'Not one quick beat of your warm heart
Nor thought that came to you apart;
Pleasure nor pity, love nor pain,
Nor sorrow has gone by in vain.' "

ROBERT LOUIS STEVENSON

Across Time's chart to lure man on, still rolls Life's sounding
    sea —
Its billows rushing mountain high — its wild winds blowing
    free;
All ports are thine, dear mariner — though others name thee
    dead,
I sight thy pennants flying, and I know thy sails are spread.
    — Emma Carleton

THE ROBERT LOUIS STEVENSON MEMORIAL IN PORTSMOUTH SQUARE

"The smelting pot of the races,"
   You called our city of old,
As we looked out through the Golden Gate
   Toward the Far East, tinged with gold.

From the South Seas came her cargoes,
   From Europe, and India's strand,
While men from all the nations
   Flocked to the new-found land.

But the shrine of all our memories,
   Of the city that is no more,
Is a golden galleon sailing
   Toward a distant, dreamy shore.

'Tis your golden ship of fancy,
   With those Christmas words below,
Bearing all the love for human kind
   That a heart like yours could know.
              — Fred Warner Carpenter

THE LAST PORTRAIT IN STEVENSON'S GALLERY

St. Ives is a character who will be treasured up in the memory along with David Balfour and Alan Breck, even with D'Artagnan and the Musketeers. — LONDON TIMES.

The tale is told: the story ends,
The last of those attractive friends,
Friends whose companionship we owe
    To that lost master of romance
With whom we fought against the foe
    Or staked the desperate chance:

Since first we tasted the delights
Of Florizel's adventurous nights,
Or paced the "Hispaniola's" deck
    And wished John Silver far away,
Or roamed the moors with Alan Breck,
    Or supped with Ballantrae.

Now bold St. Ives admittance craves
Among these fascinating knaves;
With him from prison walls we leap,
    With him our hearts to wrath are stirred,
With him we tremble, laugh, and weep,
    Until the final word.

The story ends: the tale is told,
And though new books new friends may hold,
Though Meredithians we may meet,
    Or Wessex lads with Wessex wives,
That portrait gallery is complete
    In which we place St. Ives.

THE WORD OF THE WATER

FOR THE UNVEILING OF THE STEVENSON FOUNTAIN IN SAN FRANCISCO

God made me simple from the first,
And good to quench your body's thirst.
Think you He has no ministers
To glad that wayworn soul of yours?

Here by the thronging Golden Gate
For thousands and for you I wait,
Seeing adventurous sails unfurled
For the four corners of the world.

Here passed one day, nor came again,
A prince among the tribes of men.
(For man, like me, is from his birth
A vagabond upon the earth.)

Be thankful, friend, as you pass on,
And pray for Louis Stevenson,
That by whatever trail he fare
He be refreshed in God's great care!
     — Bliss Carman

ON A YOUTHFUL PORTRAIT OF ROBERT LOUIS STEVENSON

A face of youth mature; a mouth of tender,
   Sad, human sympathy, yet something stoic
In clasp of lips: wide eyes of calmest splendour,
   And brow serenely ample and heroic; —
The features — all — lit with a soul ideal . . .
   O visionary boy! what were you seeing,
What hearing, as you stood thus midst the real
   Ere yet one master-work of yours had being?

Is it a foolish fancy that we humour —
   Investing daringly with life and spirit
This youthful portrait of you ere one rumour
   Of your great future spoke that men might hear it? —
Is it a fancy, or your first of glories,
   That you were listening, and the camera drew you
Hearing the voices of your untold stories
   And all your lovely poems calling to you?

                    — JAMES WHITCOMB RILEY

ROBERT LOUIS STEVENSON

Dear Friend, all love that love unanswered may
   I gave to thee,— my spirit leapt to thine.
   Lured by the spell of many a magic line,
I joined thy fellowship and sailed away
To golden isles, where rarest treasures lay.
   With thee, all night, I lay among the pine,
   'Mid dews and perfumes in the fresh starshine,
Till darkness moved and thrilled with coming day.

And now thou liest lone on Vaea's height,
   The visions on thine eyes we may not know.
I think of thee, awake, with keen delight,
   Hearing the forests wave, the grasses grow,
   The rush of spectral breakers far below,
Through all the starry splendour of the night!

                     — Frederic Smith

Borrow, De Quincey, the great Dean,
The sturdy leisurist Thoreau;

The furtive soul whose dark romance,
By ghostly door and haunted stair,
Explored the dusty human heart
And the forgotten garrets there;

The moralist it could not spoil,
To hold an empire in his hands;
Sir Walter, and the brood who sprang
From Homer through a hundred lands,

Singers of songs on all men's lips,
Tellers of tales in all men's ears,
Movers of hearts that still must beat
To sorrows feigned and fabled tears;

Horace and Omar, doubting still
What mystery lurks beyond the seen,
Yet blithe and reassured before
That fine unvexed Virgilian mien;

These will companion him to-night,
Beyond this iron wintry gloom,
When Shakespeare and Cervantes bid
The great joy-masters give him room.

No alien there in speech or mood,
He will pass in, one traveller more;
And portly Ben will smile to see
The velvet jacket at the door.
— BLISS CARMAN

AT THE ROAD-HOUSE: IN MEMORY OF ROBERT LOUIS STEVENSON

You hearken, fellows? Turned aside
Into the road-house of the past!
The prince of vagabonds is gone
To house among his peers at last.

The stainless gallant gentleman,
So glad of life, he gave no trace,
No hint he even once beheld
The spectre peering in his face;

But gay and modest held the road,
Nor feared the Shadow of the Dust;
And saw the whole world rich with joy,
As every valiant farer must.

I think that old and vasty inn
Will have a welcome guest to-night,
When Chaucer, breaking off some tale
That fills his hearers with delight,

Shall lift up his demure brown eyes
To bid the stranger in; and all
Will turn to greet the one on whom
The crystal lot was last to fall.

Keats of the more than mortal tongue
Will take grave Milton by the sleeve
To meet their kin, whose woven words
Had elfish music in the weave.

Dear Lamb and excellent Montaigne,
Sterne and the credible Defoe,

With the daisied turf for cover
   Where the drowsy shadows lie,
And the throstle singing over,
   And the ash against the sky,

But though in vain his yearning
   For the land he shall not greet,
And though no Spring, returning,
   Shall tempt his tarrying feet,
Though few shall weep above him,
   Or wander by his shore,
Here in the hearts that love him,
   His home is evermore.

            — Margaret Armour

IN MEMORIAM

R. L. STEVENSON

*The birds come and cry there, and twitter in the chimney,
But I go for ever and come again no more.*

Mourn for the dead, departed
    With unreturning feet;
The bright, the hero-hearted
    No comrade more shall greet;
Mourn him whom shadows cover,
    Unstricken by the years;
Mourn, Scotland, for thy lover,
    Nor stint his meed of tears.

Waft, O winds! our wailing
    Beyond the twilight verge;
In sorrow unavailing
    Chant o'er his grave your dirge!
Alack! The wand is broken,
    And mute the tragic tongue,
Ere half the words were spoken,
    Or half the song was sung.

Oh, fair may be his pillow
    'Mid waters of the West,
And blue the shining billow
    Round the haven of his rest!
But ah! the rugged mountains
    And the tempests of the north
Were dearer than the fountains
    Of the land that drew him forth.

How soft had been his sleeping
    Beneath his country's sod,
Within the quiet keeping
    Of the acre green of God,

ON BEING ASKED FOR A SONG

CONCERNING THE DEDICATION OF A MOUNTAIN IN SAMOA TO THE
MEMORY OF STEVENSON

A Letter to I. O. S.

But, friend of mine,— and his,— I am afraid!
How can I make a song
When the true song is made!
For this you say:
Because that Tusitala loved the birds,
They who named Tusitala (weaver of charmèd words —
Teller of Tales)
Have given this mountain to the birds forever!
There all day long
Bright-plumaged island-birds make gay the dales,
From off the sea the swift white bosun over the mountain sails,
From many a large-leaved tree
The gray dove cooes its low, insistent song.
They shall be absent never —
To show what love can be from man to man.
Lovers of Birds and Poets — this is glory!
It *is* a poem,— that which these Chiefs have done,—
In memory of him, the only one.
And yet our Tusitala could have sung again the pretty story—
Alas, none other can!

— RICHARD WATSON GILDER

Until the pacing watch descries
   On the sea-line a scarlet seed

Smoulder and kindle and set fire
   To the dark selvedge of the night,
The deep blue tapestry of stars,
   Then sheet the dome in pearly light,

There in perpetual tides of day,
   Where men may praise him and deplore,
The place of his lone grave shall be
   A seamark set forevermore,

High on a peak adrift with mist,
   And round whose bases, far beneath
The snow-white wheeling tropic birds,
   The emerald dragon breaks his teeth.

                — Bliss Carman

Like Arabs through the wastes of air,—
A flash, a dream, from dark to dark,—

Must feel the solemn large surmise:
By a dim vast and perilous way
We sweep through undetermined time,
Illumining this quench of clay,

A moment staunched, then forth again.
Ah, not alone you climb the steep
To set your loving burden down
Against the mighty knees of sleep.

With you we hold the sombre faith
Where creeds are sown like rain at sea;
And leave the loveliest child of earth
To slumber where he longed to be.

His fathers lit the dangerous coast
To steer the daring merchant home;
His courage lights the darkling port
Where every sea-worn sail must come.

And since he was the type of all
That strain in us which still must fare,
The fleeting migrant of a day,
Heart-high, outbound for otherwhere,

Now therefore, where the passing ships
Hang on the edges of the noon,
And Northern liners trail their smoke
Across the rising yellow moon,

Bound for his home, with shuddering screw
That beats its strength out into speed,

This savage undiscerning heart
   Is with the silent chiefs who come

To mourn their kind and bear him gifts,—
   Who kiss his hand, and take his place,
This last night he receives his friends,
   The journey-wonder on his face.

He "was not born for age." Ah no,
   For everlasting youth is his!
Part of the lyric of the earth
   With spring and leaf and blade he is.

'T will nevermore be April now
   But there will lurk a thought of him
At the street corners, gay with flowers
   From rainy valleys purple-dim.

O chiefs, you do not mourn alone!
   In that Stern North where mystery broods,
Our mother grief has many sons
   Bred in those iron solitudes.

It does not help them, to have laid
   Their coil of lightning under seas;
They are as impotent as you
   To mend the loosened wrists and knees.

And yet how many a harvest night,
   When the great luminous meteors flare
Along the trenches of the dusk,
   The men who dwell beneath the Bear,

Seeing those vagrants of the sky
   Float through the deep beyond their hark,

Into the country of your dream,
    With all your knowledge in arrears!

You who can never quite forget
    Your glimpse of Beauty as she passed,
The well-head where her knee was pressed,
    The dew wherein her foot was cast;

O you who bid the paint and clay
    Be glorious when you are dead,
And fit the plangent words in rhyme
    Where the dark secret lurks unsaid;

You brethren of the light-heart guild,
    The mystic fellowcraft of joy,
Who tarry for the news of truth,
    And listen for some vast ahoy

Blown in from sea, who crowd the wharves
    With eager eyes that wait the ship
Whose foreign tongue may fill the world
    With wondrous tales from lip to lip;

Our restless loved adventurer,
    On secret orders come to him,
Has slipped his cable, cleared the reef,
    And melted on the white sea-rim.

O granite hills, go down in blue!
    And like green clouds in opal calms,
You anchored islands of the main,
    Float up your loom of feathery palms!

For deep within your dales, where lies
    A valiant earthling stark and dumb,

Are bearing up for burial,
   Within the sun's departing ken,

The master of the roving kind.
   And there where time will set no mark
For his irrevocable rest,
   Under the spacious melting dark,

With all the nomad tented stars
   About him, they have laid him down
Above the crumbling of the sea,
   Beyond the turmoil of renown.

O all you hearts about the world
   In whom the truant gypsy blood,
Under the frost of this pale time,
   Sleeps like the daring sap and flood

That dream of April and reprieve!
   You whom the haunted vision drives,
Incredulous of home and ease,
   Perfection's lovers all your lives!

You whom the wander-spirit loves
   To lead by some forgotten clue
Forever vanishing beyond
   Horizon brinks forever new;

The road, unmarked, ordained, whereby
   Your brothers of the field and air
Before you, faithful blind and glad,
   Emerged from chaos pair by pair;

The road whereby you too must come,
   In the unvexed and fabled years,

A SEAMARK

A THRENODY FOR ROBERT LOUIS STEVENSON

Cold, the dull cold! What ails the sun,
   And takes the heart out of the day?
What makes the morning look so mean,
   The common so forlorn and gray?

The wintry city's granite heart
   Beats on in iron mockery,
And like the roaming mountain rains,
   I hear the thresh of feet go by.

It is the lonely human surf
   Surging through alleys chill with grime,
The muttering churning ceaseless floe
   Adrift out of the North of time.

Fades, it all fades! I only see
   The poster with its reds and blues,
Bidding the heart stand still to take
   Its desolating stab of news.

That intimate and magic name:
   "Dead in Samoa" . . . Cry your cries,
O city of the golden dome,
   Under the gray Atlantic skies!

But I have wander-biddings now.
   Far down the latitudes of sun,
An island mountain of the sea,
   Piercing the green and rosy zone,

Goes up into the wondrous day.
   And there the brown-limbed island men

A SAMOAN LAMENT

Groan and weep, O my heart in its sorrow!
Alas for Tusitala, who rests in the forest!
Aimlessly we wait, and sorrowing; will he again return?
Lament, O Vailima! Waiting and ever waiting!
Let us search and ask of the captains of ships,
"Be not angry, but has not Tusitala come?"

Grieve, O my heart! I cannot bear to look on
All the chiefs who are assembling.
Alas, Tusitala, thou art not here!
I look hither and thither, in vain, for thee.
— (Native)

Blow gently, thou gale of the Highland,
    Sigh softly, thou Wind of the West.

Weep low o'er the bier of thy master,
    Salt breeze
    Of the seas,
With the sound of thy sport or disaster,
    Disturb not his limitless ease.

God hath granted thy guerdon, my brother,
    And the head
    Cold and dead,
Bears the mystical crown and none other,
    And the bays on thy coffin are spread.

And the tears and the prayers of a planet,
    That start
    From the heart,
Reach over the distance and span it
    From us to the land where thou art.
        — HERMAN KNICKERBOCKER VIELE

TO ROBERT LOUIS STEVENSON

There is naught that is new, saith the Preacher;
    Death is old,
    Love is cold,
And the hate of the gods for the creature
    Waxes dull as the æons unfold.

Who shall find a new gem in the shingle,
    Tempest driven,
    Storm riven,
Where the foams of the centuries mingle
    And the seekers of jetsam have striven?

He alone of the searchers, he only,
    In the rift,
    Of the drift,
With torn hands, uncompanioned and lonely,
    Could the pearls from the nothingness sift.

O finder of infinite treasure!
    For the spoil
    Of thy moil,
Is it grateful, the respite of leisure
    That comes with the surcease of toil?

At rest are the tireless fingers
    Which for us
    From the dross
Picked the marvelous beauty that lingers
    But to tell us anew of our loss.

Sleep well in thy ocean bound island!
    Sleep and rest
    Clothe thy breast.

A GRAVE IN SAMOA

The wild birds strangely call,
And silent dawns and purple eves are here,
Where Southern stars upon his grave look down,
    Calm-eyed and wondrous clear!

No strife his resting mars!
And yet we deem far off from tropic steeps
His spirit cleaves the pathway of the storm,
    Where dark Tantallon keeps.

For still in plaintive woe,
By haunting mem'ry of his yearning led,
The wave-worn Mother of the misty strand
    Mourns for his absent dead:

Ah! bear him gently home,
To where Dunedin's streets are quaint and gray,
And ruddy lights across the steaming rains
    Shine soft at close of day!

— JOHN MACFARLANE

TO ROBERT LOUIS STEVENSON

O sailor, sailing the Unfathomed Sea,
What wind now speeds thee, and what star's thy guide?
And what adventure worth thy bravery
Calls with the lifting tide?

For thee the new coasts, gleaming, gleaming still,
For us the hope, the plunge, the engulfing night.
Oh, land! and set thy beacon on the Hill,
Our pilot into Light!

— Bruce Porter

IN MEMORIAM STEVENSON

Life's Angel shining sat in his high place
    To view the lands and waters of his globe;
A leaning Shape came through the fields of Space
    Stealthy, and touched the hem of his white robe.

The Angel turned: Brother, what ill brings thee
    Like thieving night to trespass on my day?
Yonder, Death answered him, I cannot see;
    Yonder I take this star to light my way.

                    — Owen Wister

  Memory like a rainbow stair
  Painted on the morn,
  Dearest name that on that prayer
  Christianly is borne,
  Soon to romance exhaled,
  Linger and live:
Meed no purer unto man the childlike men can give.

  Still the islands good to seek
  Rule in wonted mode;
  Let their bright surf-belted peak
  Still be thine abode!
  Grief of the loyal race
  Time shall retrieve,
And all in airy legendry thy shining spirit weave.

  To the bathers' wonder, oft
  As the night is nigh,
  And to babes beneath the soft
  Wings of lullaby
  (While we of dull unfaith,
  Thrall to our sighs,
Dual dream to quicken thee and us may not devise),

  There on summer's holy hills
  In illumined calms,
  Smile of TUSITALA thrills
  Thro' a thousand palms;
  There in rapture breaks
  Dawn on the seas,
When TUSITALA from his shoon unbinds the Pleiades.
       — Louise Imogen Guiney

Poesy, that from her breast
Strews the bay divine,
These in no natal earth
Fold him; exiled
With the wilder, gentler, he so gentle and so wild.

Aye asunder from his own
Though Samoa keep
One uplifted to her throne
Of pellucid sleep,
Winds that across the world
Ride the sea-swell,
Sign him with the tears of home, the chrism of farewell.

Was it menace from the dark,
Was it body's fret,
Early taught a patient barque
Cruises sadder yet?
Or but some primal urge
Greatly obeyed,
Drew to the unfriended hearts the heart of mercy made?

Where from water's blue outpost
Lonely Beauty calls,
Calls, and down the glowing coast
Felt denial falls;
Where tern above the cloud
Trooping, have heard
From the Prince of Welcomes by, no glad saluting word;

Where the slanted glens unbar
Boldly to the gale,
And aromas, loosed afar,
Kiss the trader's sail;
Where over lava-fire
Dances the vine,
For a symbol perfected, thy sepulchre and shrine!

FOR R. L. S. ON VAEA TOP

  Days are drooping, thought is dumb,
  Crept into a cave;
  Winter terrors thickly come
  On the haunted wave:
  Light and delight have left
  What in their stead,
Since the muses kneel about the bravely fallen head?

  Black and deadly clouds o'errush
  All our heaven in him:
  Power in many a boreal flush,
  Play of starry whim.
  Ere the king reed is cut,
  Ere the full strain,
Lo, the fickle faun is gone; the woods are bare again.

  Who are truant to the North
  Chiding, can restore?
  Which of cities, leaning forth,
  Touch him as before?
  Where serried Cant effrays
  Art, as of old,
Nevermore aloft that loved oriflamme of gold.

  Would he might indeed delay
  While the onset lowers,
  Would he had not borne away
  Ardour his and ours.
  O song upon the march
  Elsewhither blown!
The battle-dread is on us now, riding afield alone.

  Wisdom, in the motley dressed,
  Wholesome as sunshine,

VALEDICTION (R. L. S. 1894)

When from the vista of the Book I shrink,
   From lauded pens that earn ignoble wage
   Begetting nothing joyous, nothing sage,
Nor keep with Shakespeare's use one golden link;
When heavily my sanguine spirits sink
   To read too plain on each impostor page
   Only of kings the broken lineage,
Well for my peace if then on thee I think,
Louis: our priest of letters and our knight
   With whose familiar baldric hope is girt,
     From whose young hands she hears the grail away
   All glad, all great! Truer because thou wert
I am and must be, and in thy known light
   Go down to dust, content with this my day.

Louise Imogen Guiney

R. L. S., IN MEMORIAM

An elfin wight as e'er from faeryland
   Came to us straight with favour in his eyes,
   Of wondrous seed that led him to the prize
Of fancy, with the magic rod in hand.
Ah, there in faeryland we saw him stand,
   As for a while he walked with smiles and sighs,
   Amongst us, finding still the gem that buys
Delight and joy at genius's command.

And now thy place is empty: fare thee well;
   Thou livest still in hearts that owe thee more
   Than gold can reckon; for thy richer store
Is of the good that with us aye must dwell.
   Farewell; sleep sound on Vaea's windy shrine,
   While round the songsters join their songs to thine.

— A. C. R.

I. M.

R. L. S.

(1850-1894)

O, Time and Change, they range and range
    From sunshine round to thunder! —
They glance and go as the great winds blow,
    And the best of our dreams drive under:
For Time and Change estrange, estrange —
    And, now they have looked and seen us,
O, we that were dear we are all-too near
    With the thick of the world between us.

O, Death and Time, they chime and chime
    Like bells at sunset falling! —
They end the song, they right the wrong.
    They set the echoes calling:
For Death and Time bring on the prime
    Of God's own chosen weather,
And we lie in the peace of the Great Release
    As once in the grass together.

— WILLIAM ERNEST HENLEY

Take his life again
To the breast that first had warmed it,
To the tried and true,—
He has come, our well belovèd,
Scotland, back to you!
— W. Robertson Nicoll

HOME FROM THE HILL

*Home is the sailor, home from sea,
And the hunter home from the hill.* — R. L. S.

Let the weary body lie
  Where he chose its grave,
'Neath the wide and starry sky,
  By the Southern wave;
While the island holds her trust
  And the hill keeps faith,
Through the watches that divide
  The long night of death.

But the spirit, free from thrall,
  Now goes forth of these
To its birthright, and inherits
  Other lands and seas:
We shall find him when we seek him
  In an older home,—
By the hills and streams of childhood
  'Tis his weird to roam.

In the fields and woods we hear him
  Laugh and sing and sigh;
Or where by the Northern breakers
  Sea-birds troop and cry;
Or where over lonely moorlands
  Winter winds fly fleet;
Or by sunny graves he hearkens
  Voices low and sweet.

We have lost him, we have found him:
  Mother, he was fain
Nimbly to retrace his footsteps;

  God put His finger on her eyes,
   It was her tears alone that spoke.

  Now out the lights went stime by stime,
   The towns crept closer round the kirk,
  Now all the firths were smoored in rime,
   Lost winds went wailing thro' the mirk.

  A star that shot across the night
   Struck fire on Pala's mourning head,
  And left for aye a steadfast light,
   By which the mother guards her dead.

  "The lad was mine!" Erect she stands,
   No more by vain regrets oppress't,
  Once more her eyes are clear; her hands
   Are proudly crossed upon her breast.
      — JAMES MATTHEW BARRIE

'You're gey an' auld,' he cries me back,
  'That's for I like to gar you loup!'

"O' thae bit ploys he made sic books,
  A' mithers cam to watch us playing;
I feigned no to heed their looks,
  But fine I kent what they was saying!

"At times I lent him for a game
  To north and south and east and west,
But no for lang, he sune cam hame,
  For here it was he played the best.

"And when he had to cross the sea,
  He wouldna lat his een grow dim,
He bravely dree'd his weird for me,
  I tried to do the same for him.

"Ahint his face his pain was sair,
  Ahint hers grat his waefu' mither;
We kent that we should meet nae mair,
  The ane saw easy thro' the ither.

"For lang I've watched wi' trem'ling lip,
  But Louis ne'er sin syne I've seen,
The greedy island keept its grip,
  The cauldriff oceans rolled atween.

"He's deid, the ane abune the rest,
  Oh, wae, the mither left alane!
He's deid, the ane I loo'ed the best,
  Oh, mayna I hae back my nain!"

Her breast is old, it will not rise,
  Her tearless sobs in anguish choke,

50

SCOTLAND'S LAMENT

Her hands about her brows are pressed,
    She goes upon her knees to pray,
Her head is bowed upon her breast,
    And oh, she's sairly failed the day!

Her breast is old, it will not rise,
    Her tearless sobs in anguish choke,
God put His finger on her eyes,
    And then it was her tears that spoke.

"I've ha'en o' brawer sons a flow.
    My Walter mair renown could win,
And he that followed at the plough,
    But Louis was my Benjamin!

"Ye sons wha do your little best,
    Ye writing Scots, put by the pen,
He's deid, the ane abune the rest,
    I winna look at write again!

"It's sune the leave their childhood drap,
    I've ill to ken them, gaen sae grey,
But aye he climbed intil my lap,
    Or pu'd my coats to mak me play.

"He egged me on wi' mirth and prank,
    We hangit gowans on a string,
We made the doakens walk the plank,
    We mairit snails withoot the ring.

" 'I'm auld,' I pant, 'sic ploys to mak,
    To games your mither shouldna stoup.'

That you, indeed, might ever dare to be
With other praise than immortality
Unworthily content.

Not while a boy still whistles on the earth,
Not while a single human heart beats true,
Not while Love lasts, and Honour, and the Brave,
Has earth a grave,
O well-beloved, for you!

— Richard Le Gallienne

Strange craft of words, strange magic of the pen,
Whereby the dead still talk with living men;
Whereby a sentence, in its trivial scope,
May centre all we love and all we hope;
And in a couplet, like a rosebud furled,
Lie all the wistful wonder of the world.
Old are the stars, and yet they still endure,
Old are the flowers, yet never fail the spring:
Why is the song that is so old so new,
Known and yet strange each sweet small shape and hue?
How may a poet thus for ever sing,
Thus build his climbing music sweet and sure,
As builds in stars and flowers the Eternal mind?
Ah, Poet, that is yours to seek and find!
Yea, yours that magisterial skill whereby
God put all Heaven in a woman's eye,
Nature's own mighty and mysterious art
That knows to pack the whole within the part:
The shell that hums the music of the sea,
The little word big with Eternity,
The cosmic rhythm in microcosmic things —
One song the lark and one the planet sings,
One kind heart beating warm in bird and tree —
To hear it beat, who knew so well as he?

Virgil of prose! far distant is the day
When at the mention of your heartfelt name
Shall shake the head, and men, oblivious, say;
"We know him not, this master, nor his fame."
Not for so swift forgetfulness you wrought,
Day upon day, with rapt fastidious pen,
Turning, like precious stones, with anxious thought,
This word and that again and yet again,
Seeking to match its meaning with the world;
Nor to the morning stars gave ears attent,

How gladly would we spread
Impatient sails for you!

O vanished loveliness of flowers and faces,
Treasure of hair, and great immortal eyes,
Are there for these no safe and secret places?
And is it true that beauty never dies?
Soldiers and saints, haughty and lovely names,
Women who set the whole wide world in flames,
Poets who sang their passion to the skies,
And lovers wild and wise:
Fought they and prayed for some poor flitting gleam,
Was all they loved and worshipped but a dream?
Is Love a lie and fame indeed a breath,
And is there no sure thing in life — but death?
Or may it be, within that guarded shore,
He meets Her now whom I shall meet no more
Till kind Death fold me 'neath his shadowy wing:
She whom within my heart I softly tell
That he is dead whom once we loved so well,
He, the immortal master whom I sing.

Immortal! Yea, dare we the word again,
If aught remaineth of our mortal day,
That which is written — shall it not remain?
That which is sung, is it not built for aye?
Faces must fade, for all their golden looks,
Unless some poet them eternalize,
Make live those golden looks in golden books;
Death, soon or late, will quench the brightest eyes —
'Tis only what is written never dies.
Yea, memories that guard like sacred gold
Some sainted face, they also must grow old,
Pass and forget, and think — or darest thou not! —
On all the beauty that is quite forgot.

And Death is but the pilot come aboard.
Methinks I see him smile a boy's glad smile
On maddened winds and waters, reefs unknown,
As thunders in the sail the dread typhoon,
And in the surf the shuddering timbers groan;
Horror ahead, and Death beside the wheel:
Then — spreading stillness of the broad lagoon,
And lap of waters round the resting keel.

Strange Isle of Voices! must we ask in vain,
In vain beseech and win no answering word,
Save mocking echoes of our lonely pain
From lonely hill and bird?
Island beneath whose unrelenting coast,
As though it never in the sun had been,
The whole world's treasure lieth sunk and lost,
Unsunned, unseen.
For, either sunk beyond the diver's skill,
There, fathoms deep, our gold is all arust,
Or in that island it is hoarded still.
Yea, some have said, within thy dreadful wall
There is a folk that know not death at all,
The loved we lost, the lost we love, are there.
Will no kind voice make answer to our cry,
Give to our aching hearts some little trust,
Show how 'tis good to live, but best to die?
Some voice that knows
Whither the dead man goes:
We hear his music from the other side,
Maybe a little tapping on the door,
A something called, a something sighed —
No more.
O for some voice to valiantly declare
The best news true!
Then, Happy Island of the Happy Dead,

ROBERT LOUIS STEVENSON

AN ELEGY

High on his Patmos of the Southern Seas
Our northern dreamer sleeps,
Strange stars above him, and above his grave
Strange leaves and wings their tropic splendours wave,
While, far beneath, mile after shimmering mile,
The great Pacific, with its faery deeps,
Smiles all day long its silken secret smile.

Son of a race nomadic, finding still
Its home in regions furthest from its home,
Ranging untired the borders of the world,
And resting but to roam;
Loved of his land, and making all his boast
The birthright of the blood from which he came,
Heir to those lights that guard the Scottish coast,
And caring only for a filial fame;
Proud, if a poet, he was Scotsman most,
And bore a Scottish name.

Death, that long sought our poet, finds at last,
Death, that pursued him over land and sea:
Not his the flight of fear, the heart aghast
With stony dread of immortality,
He fled "not cowardly";
Fled, as some captain, in whose shaping hand
Lies the momentous fortunes of his land,
Sheds not vainglorious blood upon the field,
But dares to fly — yea! even dares to yield.
Death! why at last he finds his treasure isle,
And he the pirate of its hidden hoard;
Life! 'twas the ship he sailed to seek it in,

ROBERT LOUIS STEVENSON

Wondrous as though a star with twofold light
   Should fill her lamp for either hemisphere,
   Piercing cold skies with scintillation clear
While glowing on the sultry Southern night,
Was miracle of him who could unite
   Pine and the purple harbour of the deer
   With palm-plumed islets that sequestered hear
The far-off wave their zoning coral smite.

Still roars the surf, still bounds the herd, but where
   Is one to hear, and see, and tell again?
As dancers pause on an arrested air
   Stand the fleet creatures of his fruitful brain
In shade and sadness, dumb as the despair
   Of Britain mourning for her bard in vain.
                    — RICHARD GARNETT

ROBERT LOUIS STEVENSON

Why need we mourn his loss?
   His name is with the great;
Close to the Southern Cross
   He sleeps in matchless state.

Softly the stars shall shower
   Their dewy brilliancies;
And many a Southern flower
   Shall climb his grave to kiss.

Far down the murmuring river
   Shall join the murmuring surge;
The haunted winds for ever
   Shall chant his mountain-dirge.

In darkness and in light,
   Until the Crack of Doom,
The morning and the night
   Shall watch about his tomb.

High over field and fountain,
   Far in a place apart,
He sleeps on Pala Mountain:
   He lives in every heart.
              — JOHN DAVIDSON

R. L. S.

Home is the sailor, home from sea:
  Her far-borne canvas furled,
The ship pours shining on the quay
  The plunder of the world.

Home is the hunter from the hill:
  Fast in the boundless snare
All flesh lies taken at his will
  And every fowl of air.

'Tis evening on the moorland free,
  The starlit wave is still:
Home is the sailor from the sea,
  The hunter from the hill.
— A. E. Housman

Yea, gladly grant you, with a generous hand,
Far glimpses of the winding, wind-swept strand,
The glens and mountains of your native land,

Until you hear the pipes upon the breeze —
But wake unto the wild realities,
The tangled forests and the boundless seas!

For lo! the moonless night has passed away,
A sudden dawn dispels the shadows grey,
The glad sea moves and hails the quickening day.

New life within the arbours of your fief
Awakes the blossom, quivers in the leaf,
And splendour flames upon the coral reef.

If such a prospect stimulate your art,
More than our meadows where the shadows dart,
More than the life which throbs in London's heart,

Then stay, encircled by your Southern bowers,
And weave, amid the incense of the flowers,
The skein of fair romance — the gain is ours!

— F. J. Cox

GREETING

(TO ROBERT LOUIS STEVENSON, IN SAMOA)

We, pent in cities, prisoned in the mart,
Can know you only as a man apart,
But ever-present through your matchless art.

You have exchanged the old, familiar ways
For isles, where, through the range of splendid days,
Her treasure Nature lavishly displays.

There, by the gracious sweep of ampler seas,
That swell responsive to the odorous breeze,
You have the wine of Life, and we the lees!

You mark, perchance, within your island bowers,
The slow departure of the languorous hours,
And breathe the sweetness of the strange wild-flowers,

And everything your soul and sense delights —
But in the solemn wonder of your nights,
When Peace her message on the landscape writes;

When Ocean scarcely flecks her marge with foam —
Your thoughts must sometimes from your island roam,
To centre on the sober face of Home.

Though many a league of water rolls between
The simple beauty of an English scene,
From all these wilder charms your love may wean.

Some kindly sprite may bring you as a boon
Sweets from the rose that crowns imperial June,
Or reminiscence of the throstle's tune;

IV

Vanish'd? Ay, that's still the trouble,
                    Tusitala.
Though your tropic isle rejoices,
'Tis to us an Isle of Voices
Hollow like the elfin double
Cry of disembodied echoes,
Or an owlet's wicked laughter,
Or the cold and hornèd gecko's
Croaking from a ruined rafter,—
Voices these of things existing,
Yet incessantly resisting
Eyes and hands that follow after;
You are circled, as by magic,
In a surf-built palmy bubble,
                    Tusitala;
Fate hath chosen, but the choice is
Half delectable, half tragic,
For we hear you speak, like Moses,
And we greet you back, enchanted,
But reply's no sooner granted,
Than the rifted cloudland closes.

— EDMUND GOSSE

Ah! but does your heart remember,
                              Tusitala,
Westward in our Scotch September,
Blue against the pale sun's ember,—
That low rim of faint long islands,
Barren, granite-snouted nesses,
Plunging in the dull'd Atlantic,
Where beyond Tiree one guesses
At the full tide, loud and frantic?

III

By strange pathways God hath brought you,
                              Tusitala,
In strange webs of fortune caught you,
Led you by strange moods and measures
To this paradise of pleasures!
And the body-guard that sought you
To conduct you home to glory,—
Dark the oriflammes they carried,
In the mist their cohort tarried,—
They were Languor, Pain, and Sorrow,
                              Tusitala!
Scarcely we endured their story
Trailing on from morn to morrow,
Such the devious roads they led you,
Such the error, such the vastness,
Such the cloud that overspread you,
Under the exile bow'd and banish'd,
Lost, like Moses in the fastness,
Till we almost deem'd you vanished.

TO TUSITALA IN VAILIMA

I

Clearest voice in Britain's chorus,
                        Tusitala!
Years ago, years four-and-twenty,
Grey and cloudland drifted o'er us,
When these ears first heard you talking,
When these eyes first saw you smiling.
Years of famine, years of plenty,
Years of beckoning and beguiling,
Years of yielding, shifting, baulking,—
When the good ship "Clansman" bore us
Round the spits of Tobermory,
Glens of Voulin like a vision,
Crags of Knoidart, huge and hoary,—
We had laughed in light derision,
Had they told us, told the daring
                        Tusitala,
What the years' pale hands were bearing,—
Years in stately dim division.

II

Now the skies are pure above you,
                        Tusitala;
Feather'd trees bow down to love you;
Perfum'd winds from shining waters
Stir the sanguine-leav'd hibiscus
That your kingdom's dusk-ey'd daughters
Weave about their shining tresses;
Dew-fed guavas drop their viscous
Honey at the sun's caresses,
Where eternal summer blesses
Your ethereal musky highlands;—

WRITTEN IN A COPY OF MR. STEVENSON'S
CATRIONA

Glorious Sir Walter, Shakespeare's brother brain,
  Fortune's invincible victor-victim, Scott,
  Mere lettered fame, 'tis said, esteeming not,
Save as it ministered to weightier gain,
Had yet his roseate dream, though dreamed in vain;
  The dream that, crowning his terrestrial lot,
  A race of great and splendid heirs, begot
Of his own loins, o'er Abbotsford should reign.

Fate spurned his wish, but promised, in amends,
  One mighty scion of his heart and mind:
    And where far isles the languid ocean fleck,—
  Flying the cold kiss of our northern wind,—
Lo, the rare spirit through whom we hail as friends
    The immortal Highland maid and Alan Breck!
               — WILLIAM WATSON

O Louis, you that writes in Scots,
Ye're far awa' frae stirks and stots,
Wi' drookit hurdies, tails in knots,
  An unco way!
My mirth's like thorns aneth the pots
  In Ballantrae!

— ANDREW LANG

BALLANT O' BALLANTRAE

TO ROBERT LOUIS STEVENSON

Written in wet weather, this conveyed to the Master of Ballantrae a wrong idea of a very beautiful and charming place, with links, a river celebrated by Burns, good sea-fishing, and, on the river, a ruined castle at every turn of the stream. "Try Ballantrae" is a word of wisdom.

Whan suthern wunds gar spindrift flee
Abune the clachan, faddums hie,
Whan for the cluds I canna see
   The bonny lift,
I'd fain indite an Ode to *thee*
   Had I the gift!

Ken ye the coast o' wastland Ayr?
Oh mon, it's unco bleak and bare!
Ye daunder here, ye daunder there,
   And mak' your moan,
They've rain and wund eneuch to tear
   The suthern cone!

Ye're seekin' sport! There's nane ava',
Ye'll sit and glower ahint the wa'
At bleesin' breakers till ye staw,
   If that's yer wush;
"There's aye the Stinchar." Hoot awa',
   She wunna fush!

She wunna fush at ony gait,
She's roarin' reid in wrathfu' spate;
Maist like yer Kimmer when ye're late
   Frae Girvan Fair!
Forbye to speer for leave I'm blate
   For fushin' there!

  To half believe them;
And, stamped wi' *Tusitala's* name,
  They'll a' receive them.

And folk to come ayont the sea
May hear the yowl o' the Banshie,
And frae the water-kelpie flee,
  Ere a' things cease,—
And island bairns may stolen be
  By the Folk o' Peace.
— A<small>NDREW</small> L<small>ANG</small>

TO ROBERT LOUIS STEVENSON

With Kirk's "Secret Commonwealth"

O Louis! you that like them maist,
Ye're far frae kelpie, wraith, and ghaist,
And fairy dames, no unco chaste,
   And haunted cell.
Among a heathen clan ye're placed,
   That kensna hell!

Ye hae nae heather, peat, nor birks,
Nae trout in a' yer burnies lurks,
There are nae bonny U. P. kirks,
   An awfu' place!
Nane kens the Covenant o' Works
   Frae that o' Grace.

But whiles, maybe, to them ye'll read
Blads o' the Covenanting creed,
And while their pagan wames ye'll feed
   On halesome parritch;
And syne ye'll gar them learn a screed
   O' the Shorter Carritch.

Yet thae uncovenanted shavers
Hae rowth, ye say, o' clash and clavers
O' gods and etins — auld wives' havers,
   But their delight;
The voice o' him that tells them quavers
   Just wi' fair fright.

And ye might tell, ayont the faem,
Thae Hieland clashes o' our hame
To speak the truth, I takna shame

TO PROSPERO IN SAMOA

A world away in dreams we roam —
   The tempest howls, the lightnings fall;
Slim rainbows span the leaping foam
   That shatters on your fortress wall;
Yet forth to shipwreck would we go
To be the guests of Prospero:

To join your court where glints the blue
   Through frets of lank banana fans —
Mirandas, but of warmer hue,
   And other, lazier Calibans,
And beaded Ariel-eyes that glow
To list the tale of Prospero.

They stoop from sultry southern stars,
   They rise from yonder Peaceful Sea,
The sprites you bind in mystic bars
   On Fancy's page, your thralls, as we.
A dream! — we wake, and falling snow
Hides Treasure Isle and Prospero.

Then flash us tidings of your weal!
   Bid Ariel tread the ocean floor,
And fire-fed dragons, ribbed with steel,
   Rush treasure-freighted to our shore
With tales of mingled mirth and woe,
The magic scroll of Prospero!
— Y. Y.

Ah! the pig-tailed, quidding pirates and the pretty pranks we played,
All have since been put a stop-to by the naughty Board of Trade;
The schooners and the merry crews are laid away to rest,
A little south the sunset in the Islands of the Blest.

— JOHN MASEFIELD

A BALLAD OF JOHN SILVER

We were schooner-rigged and rakish, with a long and lissome hull,
And we flew the pretty colours of the cross-bones and the skull;
We'd a big black Jolly Roger flapping grimly at the fore,
And we sailed the Spanish Water in the happy days of yore.

We'd a long brass gun amidships, like a well-conducted ship,
We had each a brace of pistols and a cutlass at the hip;
It's a point which tells against us, and a fact to be deplored,
But we chased the goodly merchant-men and laid their ships aboard.

Then the dead men fouled the scuppers and the wounded filled the chains,
And the paint-work all was spattered with other people's brains,
She was boarded, she was looted, she was scuttled till she sank,
And the pale survivors left us by the medium of the plank.

O! then it was (while standing by the taffrail on the poop)
We could hear the drowning folk lament the absent chicken-coop;
Then, having washed the blood away, we'd little else to do
Than dance a quiet hornpipe as the old salts taught us to.

O! the fiddle on the fo'c's'le, and the slapping naked soles,
And the genial "Down the middle, Jake, and curtsey when she rolls!"
With the silver seas around us and the pale moon overhead,
And the lookout not a-looking and his pipe-bowl glowing red.

And the lace stiff-dry in a purplish blot.
   Or was she wench . . .
    Or some shuddering maid . . ?
  That dared the knife
   And that took the blade!
By God! She was stuff for a plucky jade —
 Yo-ho-ho and a bottle of rum!

Fifteen men on the dead man's chest —
 Yo-ho-ho and a bottle of rum!
Drink and the devil had done for the rest —
 Yo-ho-ho and a bottle of rum!
We wrapped 'em all in a mains'l tight,
With twice ten turns of the hawser's bight,
And we heaved 'em over and out of sight —
  With a yo-heave-ho!
   And a fare-you-well!
  And a sullen plunge
   In the sullen swell —
Ten fathoms deep on the road to hell —
 Yo-ho-ho and a bottle of rum!

      — YOUNG E. ALLISON

Fifteen men of 'em stiff and stark —
   Yo-ho-ho and a bottle of rum!
Ten of the crew had the murder mark —
   Yo-ho-ho and a bottle of rum!
'Twas a cutlass swipe, or an ounce of lead,
Or a yawing hole in a battered head,
And the scuppers glut with a rotting red.
       And there they lay —
          Aye, damn my eyes! —
       All lookouts clapped
         On paradise —
All souls bound just contrariwise —
   Yo-ho-ho and a bottle of rum!

Fifteen men of 'em good and true —
   Yo-ho-ho and a bottle of rum!
Every man jack could ha' sailed with Old Pew —
   Yo-ho-ho and a bottle of rum!
There was chest on chest full of Spanish gold,
With a ton of plate in the middle hold,
And the cabins riot of stuff untold.
       And they lay there
         That had took the plum,
       With sightless glare
         And their lips struck dumb,
While we shared all by the rule of thumb —
   Yo-ho-ho and a bottle of rum!

More was seen through the sternlight screen —
   Yo-ho-ho and a bottle of rum!
Chartings ondoubt where a woman had been —
   Yo-ho-ho and a bottle of rum!
A flimsy shift on a bunker cot,
With a thin dirk slot through the bosom spot

DERELICT

A REMINISCENCE OF "TREASURE ISLAND"

Fifteen men on the dead man's chest —
Yo-ho-ho and a bottle of rum!
Drink and the devil had done for the rest —
Yo-ho-ho and a bottle of rum!
    (Cap'n Billy Bones his song)

Fifteen men on the dead man's chest —
 Yo-ho-ho and a bottle of rum!
Drink and the devil had done for the rest —
 Yo-ho-ho and a bottle of rum!
The mate was fixed by the bos'n's pike,
The bos'n brained with a marlinspike,
And Cookey's throat was marked belike
  It had been gripped
   By fingers ten;
  And there they lay,
   All good dead men,
Like break-o'-day in a boozing-ken —
 Yo-ho-ho and a bottle of rum!

Fifteen men of a whole ship's list —
 Yo-ho-ho and a bottle of rum!
All of 'em down from the devil's own fist —
 Yo-ho-ho and a bottle of rum!
The skipper lay with his nob in gore
Where the scullion's axe his cheek had shore —
And the scullion he was stabbed times four.
  And there they lay,
   And the soggy skies
  Dripped all day long
   In up-staring eyes —
At murk sunset and at foul sunrise —
 Yo-ho-ho and a bottle of rum!

STEVENSON'S "UNDERWOODS"

"How do I like 'Underwoods'?"
As I like all piquant foods,—
Drupe and kernel, flavors, scents,
Thorny thick and brake dispense;
Scarlet haws and cherries black;
Ground-nuts that of earth do smack;
Sweet-birch browsings, sassafras;
Strawberries in the sleekest grass;
Sippings from the clover's horn,
On a luscious dew-drowned morn;
May-apples with jellied core,
And the oaks' wild honey store.

How do I like "Underwoods"?
As I like the flickering moods
Sun and wind at evening rouse
Elfishly among the boughs;
Greening showers in fitful drops,
Thrushes singing in the stops;
Stars in day-time, spirit-keen,
Up a glade's sky-window seen;
Lonesome forest sounds unkenned,
That would Grief or Fancy friend,
Straying through the solitudes,—
Thus do I like "Underwoods"!

— Edith M. Thomas

TO R. L. S.

A Child,
Curious and innocent,
Slips from his Nurse, and rejoicing
Loses himself in the Fair.

Thro' the jostle and din
Wandering, he revels,
Dreaming, desiring, possessing;
Till, of a sudden
Tired and afraid, he beholds
The sordid assemblage
Just as it is; and he runs
With a sob to his Nurse
(Lighting at last on him),
And in her motherly bosom
Cries him to sleep.

Thus thro' the World,
Seeing and feeling and knowing,
Goes Man: till at last,
Tired of experience, he turns
To the friendly and comforting breast
Of the old nurse, Death.

— WILLIAM ERNEST HENLEY

TO ROBERT LOUIS STEVENSON

ON HIS FIRST VISIT TO AMERICA

Robert Louis Stevenson!
Blue the lift and braw the dawn
O' yer comin' here amang
Strangers wha hae luved ye lang!
Strangers tae ye we maun be,
Yet tae us ye're kenned a wee
By the writin's ye hae done,
Robert Louis Stevenson.

Syne ye've pit yer pen tae sic'
Tales it stabbt us tae the quick —
Whiles o' tropic isles an' seas
An' o' gowden treesuries —
Tales o' deid men's banes; an' tales
Swete as sangs o' nightingales
When the nune o' mirk's begun —
Robert Louis Stevenson.

Sae we hail thee! nane the less
For the "burr" that ye caress
Wi' yer denty tongue o' Scots,
Makin' words forget-me-nots
O' yer bonnie braes that were
Sung o' Burns the Poemer —
And that later lavrock, one
Robert Louis Stevenson.

— James Whitcomb Riley

TO ROBERT LOUIS STEVENSON

Because the way is long, and we may never
    Meet face to face this side the shadowed land;
    Because — a thousand things! — because the hand
May seek in friendly, but in vain, endeavour
Some dreamed-of clasp; because, though seas may sever
    This kindred-seeking dust, there is no strand
    Too far for loving thoughts — spread wave or sand,
For evermore, thought scorneth them for ever: —
    Therefore lest fate hold by her barrier still,
        No kindlier proving, hence, than in the past —
        Lest on that unknown bourn there is no meeting,—
    For thee, upon the tide of good and ill
        Which floods with ceaseless flow this world, I cast
        This waif: for thee, brave heart, my soul's best greeting.

                  — ROBERT BURNS WILSON

"KIDNAPPED"

A graphic story here you'll find by R. L. Stevenson.
It beats the *Treasure Island* — or any he has done!
From opening unto finish your attention's kept alive —
The scene is laid in Scotland just after 'Forty-five —
'Tis a tale of wild adventure most marvelously told,
And cunningly the writer does his clever plot unfold:
Throughout the narrative we find the author at his best,
'Tis full of fights and bustle and of thrilling interest;
The characters are drawn, you'll find, with most consummate skill,—
A book you ought at once to read, and read at once you will!

APPARITION

Thin-legged, thin-chested, slight unspeakably,
Neat-footed and weak-fingered: in his face —
Lean, large-boned, curved of beak, and touched with race,
Bold-lipped, rich-tinted, mutable as the sea,
The brown eyes radiant with vivacity —
There shines a brilliant and romantic grace,
A spirit intense and rare, with trace on trace
Of passion, impudence and energy.

Valiant in velvet, light in ragged luck,
Most vain, most generous, sternly critical,
Buffoon and poet, lover and sensualist:
A deal of Ariel, just a streak of Puck,
Much Antony, of Hamlet most of all,
And something of the Shorter-Catechist.

— WILLIAM ERNEST HENLEY

IN PRAISE OF STEVENSON

OVER THE SEA TO SKYE

Sing me a song of a lad that is gone,
Say, could that lad be I?
Merry of soul he sailed on a day
Over the sea to Skye.

Mull was astern, Egg on the port,
Rum on the starboard bow;
Glory of youth glowed in his soul:
Where is that glory now?

Sing me a song of a lad that is gone,
Say, could that lad be I?
Merry of soul he sailed on a day
Over the sea to Skye.

Give me again all that was there,
Give me the sun that shone!
Give me the eyes, give me the soul,
Give me the lad that's gone!

Sing me a song of a lad that is gone,
Say, could that lad be I?
Merry of soul he sailed on a day
Over the sea to Skye.

Billow and breeze, islands and seas,
Mountains of rain and sun,
All that was good, all that was fair,
All that was me is gone.
— ROBERT LOUIS STEVENSON

From *Poems and Ballads*; copyright, 1895, 1913, by Charles Scribner's Sons. By permission of the publishers.

It has been interesting to note how Stevenson's philosophy of life has impressed and inspired many of the poets; notably that admirable doctrine, "To travel hopefully is a better thing than to arrive." And it has been keenly moving to realize how many, with the poet's vision, have seen (as how could they fail to see?) in certain of his own poems — so appallingly clairvoyant, it seems, now that he is dead — the tragedy and triumph of his life, and have felt the often whimsical resignation of the man in the face of Doom. His most fantastic thoughts were written, as it were, while Death stood behind the chair and chuckled. It is obvious, indeed, that life was for him the curious and grotesque spectacle he often made it, for the very reason that he viewed the merry-go-round from an invalid's chair.

The arrangement of poems is as nearly chronological as is possible from information at hand; and the labour of collecting, comparing and authenticating has been very truly a labour of love. While I have added yet another volume to the already considerable number which catalogue as Stevensoniana, I feel that no apology need be made for one more, so little of which is my own, so much of which is Stevenson's.

VINCENT STARRETT

be asserted that he was one of the best story-tellers who have written in our language. To his high narrative and dramatic faculty, he joined qualities of humour, insight, sympathy and style, rare among English story-writers of whatever rank. But the superficial judgment which sets him down as a story-teller is as narrow as that which would make of him merely a stylist, or that which finds his finest performance in his essays. I think no one as yet has ventured to remark that his genius reached its zenith in his poetry, graceful and delightful and poignant as much of it is, although it would be no surprise to learn that this, too, had been claimed for him. The truth is, he handled supremely well so wide a range of literary forms, that the commentator who blandly seeks to bestow the critical accolade on a single count only succeeds in making himself ridiculous. The proverbial pendulum still oscillates gently; when it shall have ceased to swing, Stevenson, I believe, will be found to occupy a loftier place than many critics now are willing to accord him, if somewhat lower than that forced upon him by unbridled enthusiasts. And, as now, with the uncritical many, who care not a jot one way or the other, he will still be Louis, the Beloved, "Tusitala, the Teller of Tales." Happy all who share this reckless enthusiasm!

Some notion of Stevenson's wide popularity, if additional evidence be necessary, is obtained from the number and the passion of tributes to him, both in his lifetime and since his death. Naturally, there are more of the latter than of the former. In the present compilation, I have attempted to collect in one set of covers, all the better known tributes in verse, and such other verses composed in his honour or around his fame as became accessible by diligent research; together with poems inspired by his writings, and other material that might fairly be included in this, I believe, the first anthology of the subject. The poems thus brought together are not of uniform excellence, but I venture to assert that in sympathy and sincerity the slightest is unsurpassed by the finest.

INTRODUCTION

R. L. S. . . "These familiar initials are, I suppose, the best beloved in recent literature," wrote J. M. Barrie, in *Margaret Ogilvy*; "certainly they are the sweetest to me."

To this tribute, an overwhelming chorus has answered, "And to me!"

Indeed, in the long line of immortals, few have been rendered such universal and sincere homage as the lean Scotsman, whose courage no less than his genius has endeared him to all who love a brave tale and a brave man. But even genius which compels admiration seldom enough inspires love; and that Stevenson was — and is — loved, is beyond all dispute. The phenomenon, then, is born of the man himself, and the romantic colours of his life. His long quest after health, his unfailing cheerfulness and courage, his early and tragic death, and his remote yet triumphant tomb on Vaea top, fire the imagination like one of his own tales. His stories obviously are the man. Given health and strength, the invincible invalid would have lived them; failing that, he wrote them down in words of inimitable wonder.

An enormous literature has grown up around the name and fame of Louis Stevenson. Of late, there has been a critical tendency toward the apostate mood of Henley, on a famous occasion, but we may fairly suppose it to mark the inevitable reaction after years of tumultuous and not always judicious adulation. Henley's memorable article has done more good than harm, for, as Mr. J. A. Hammerton remarks, "it is salutary to remember that Stevenson was a little lower than the angels." The time certainly has come, however, when it may

THE TRAVELLERS	127
Michael Monahan	
A HOUSE IN SARANAC	128
George Steele Seymour	
THE PASSING OF LOUIS	130
Vincent Starrett	
ADVENTURING WITH R. L. S.	132
Ethel Feuerlicht	
ACKNOWLEDGMENTS	133
NOTES	135

R. L. S.	107
Edmund Gosse	
PARAPHRASE	108
Frederic Smith	
R. L. S.	109
Frederic Smith	
"TREASURE ISLAND"	110
Bert Leston Taylor	
TREASURE ISLAND	111
Patrick Chalmers	
THE OLD VAQUERO REMEMBERS ROBERT LOUIS STEVENSON	112
Reginald Rogers	
AT THE ROBERT LOUIS STEVENSON FOUNTAIN	113
John Northern Hilliard	
LONG JOHN SILVER	115
Vincent Starrett	
TO R. L. S.	116
R. R. Greenwood	
ROBERT LOUIS STEVENSON	117
Ethel Talbot Scheffauer	
TO ROBERT LOUIS STEVENSON	118
Edwin Carlile Litsey	
FRIEND O' MINE	119
Stephen Chalmers	
THE DEATH OF FLINT	121
Stephen Chalmers	
ROBERT LOUIS STEVENSON	123
Stephen Chalmers	
SAINT R. L. S.	124
Sarah N. Cleghorn	
ON CERTAIN CRITICS OF STEVENSON	125
Vincent Starrett	
SAMOA AND R. L. S.	126
Jesse Edgar Middleton	

STEVENSON'S BIRTHDAY	89
Katherine Miller	
R. L. S., IN MEMORIAM	90
Austin Dobson	
R. L. STEVENSON	91
C. P. Nettleton	
STEVENSON-NICHOLSON	92
C. de Fornaro	
AT THE STEVENSON FOUNTAIN	93
Wallace Irwin	
TO R. L. S.	94
Charles W. Collins	
TO R. L. S.	95
Alfred Austin	
THE BURIAL OF ROBERT LOUIS STEVENSON AT SAMOA .	96
Florence Earle Coates	
ON A PORTRAIT OF "R. L. S." THE INVALID . . .	97
Arthur Stringer	
TO STEVENSON	98
Charles Keeler	
TUSITALA: TELLER OF TALES	99
Mary H. Krout	
STEVENSON	100
George Edgar Montgomery	
R. L. S.	101
Arthur Johnstone	
ROBERT LOUIS STEVENSON	102
Lizette Woodworth Reese	
THOUGHT OF STEVENSON	103
Arthur Upson	
LEGEND OF PORTSMOUTH SQUARE	104
W. O. McGeeham	
TOASTS IN A LIBRARY	106
Anonymous	

A Seamark	66
Bliss Carman	
On Being Asked for a Song	72
Richard Watson Gilder	
In Memoriam, R. L. Stevenson	73
Margaret Armour	
At the Road House: In Memory of Robert Louis Stevenson	75
Bliss Carman	
Robert Louis Stevenson	77
Frederic Smith	
On a Youthful Portrait of Robert Louis Stevenson	78
James Whitcomb Riley	
The Word of the Water	79
Bliss Carman	
The Last Portrait in Stevenson's Gallery . .	80
St. James Gazette	
The Robert Louis Stevenson Memorial in Portsmouth Square	81
Fred Warner Carpenter	
Robert Louis Stevenson	82
Emma Carleton	
Inscription	83
Selected	
Stevenson of the Letters	84
B. Paul Neuman	
"Tusitala"	85
P. T. M.	
To Stevenson	86
Grace W. Hazard	
A Toast to Tusitala	87
Bliss Carman	
To Robert Louis Stevenson	88
Richard Burton	

To Tusitala in Vailima . . . . Edmund Gosse	36
Greeting . . . . F. J. Cox	39
R. L. S. . . . . A. E. Housman	41
Robert Louis Stevenson . . . . . . John Davidson	42
Robert Louis Stevenson . . . . . . Richard Garnett	43
Robert Louis Stevenson: An Elegy . . . Richard Le Gallienne	44
Scotland's Lament . . . . James Matthew Barrie	49
Home From the Hill . . . . W. Robertson Nicoll	52
I. M., R. L. S. . . . . William Ernest Henley	54
R. L. S., In Memoriam . . . . . . A. C. R.	55
Valediction . . . . Louise Imogen Guiney	56
For R. L. S. on Vaea Top . . . . . . Louise Imogen Guiney	57
In Memoriam Stevenson . . . . . . Owen Wister	60
To Robert Louis Stevenson . . . . . Bruce Porter	61
A Grave in Samoa . . . . J. Macfarlane	62
To Robert Louis Stevenson . . . . . Herman Knickerbocker Viele	63
A Samoan Lament . . . . Native	65

CONTENTS

INTRODUCTION	13
OVER THE SEA TO SKYE	16
APPARITION	19
William Ernest Henley	
"KIDNAPPED"	20
Punch	
TO ROBERT LOUIS STEVENSON	21
Robert Burns Wilson	
TO ROBERT LOUIS STEVENSON ON HIS FIRST VISIT TO	
AMERICA	22
James Whitcomb Riley	
TO R. L. S.	23
Willam Ernest Henley	
STEVENSON'S "UNDERWOODS"	24
Edith M. Thomas	
DERELICT	25
Young E. Allison	
A BALLAD OF JOHN SILVER	28
John Masefield	
TO PROSPERO IN SAMOA	30
Y. Y.	
TO ROBERT LOUIS STEVENSON	31
Andrew Lang	
BALLANT O' BALLANTRAE	33
Andrew Lang	
WRITTEN IN A COPY OF MR. STEVENSON'S "CATRIONA"	35
William Watson	

To
Walter M. Hill
A Prince of Bookfellows

Three hundred twenty-five copies of this first edition have been printed from type in November, 1919, of which three hundred copies are for sale to Bookfellows

Copyright 1919 by
Flora Warren Seymour

THE TORCH PRESS
CEDAR RAPIDS
IOWA

In Praise of Stevenson

An Anthology

Edited, with an Introduction
and Notes, by
Vincent Starrett

CHICAGO
THE BOOKFELLOWS
1919

The Bookfellow Series
Volume One

In Praise of Stevenson